THE BEST DULCIMER METHOD YET

by ALBERT GAMSE

Duet, Rhythm and Finger Picking Arrangements
by STEVE SECHAK
Illustrated by ANNA STAJDUHAR

T0083415

The 3-string Dulcimer has one string for melodies. The 4-string Dulcimer has a double string for melodies. The other strings are merely harmonizing "drone" sounds. Because of its simplicity, it is generally regarded as an instrument with a very limited repertoire. Disproving this, we have included in this book 139 familiar tunes in various categories of music, which are playable and effective on this instrument.

It is generally associated with the southern Appalachian region of the United States but its origin dates back hundreds of years. It has been linked to ancient Asiatic instruments. Known as the "Dowcemere", it has been a favorite instrument of the southern English highlands. Among early German musical instruments, it is known as the "Scheitholt". The French associate it with the Vosges mountain district, calling it "Epinette des Vosges". Norwegians refer to a similar instrument of the 17th century, the "Langeleik". It is mentioned in 12th century poetry! So no-one can really pin-point its real origin.

As various settlers came to the United States from the old world, they brought with them numerous old and varied musical instruments. The Appalachian "Dulcimer" just happened to emerge. As its name implies, the "Dulcimer" (Latin "dulcis" for "sweet" and Greek "melos" for "song") produces a "sweet song" with a haunting droning sound reminiscent of Scottish bagpipes.

Irrespective of its origin, this instrument is now at your service and should afford you considerable enjoyment. Take care of it! The Dulcimer should be kept away from excessive dampness or heat. Give it an occasional waxing to help protect the finish.

THE PUBLISHER

© Copyright MCMLXXIV by Lewis Music Publishing Co., Inc.
263 Veterans Boulevard, Carlstadt, N.J. 07072

International Copyright Secured   Made in U.S.A.

2

CONTENTS

ABBREVIATIONS IN CLASSIFIED SONG INDEX:
(See special index, foot of page 3)

(D) Descant (songs with counter-melodies)
(R) Rhythm effects (F) Finger Picking
(M) Songs with MINOR TUNING

SELECTIONS

THE DULCIMER AND ITS COMPONENT PARTS

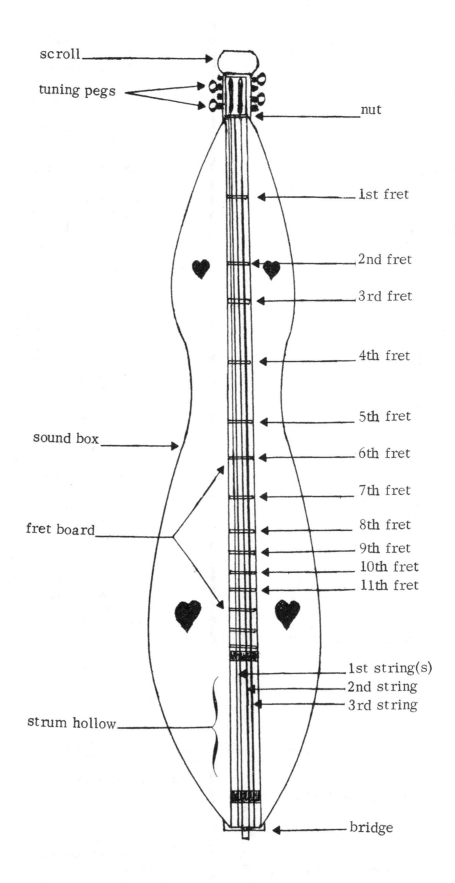

scroll

tuning pegs

nut

1st fret

2nd fret

3rd fret

4th fret

5th fret

sound box

6th fret

7th fret

8th fret

fret board

9th fret

10th fret

11th fret

1st string(s)

2nd string

3rd string

strum hollow

bridge

HOW TO PLAY THE DULCIMER

DESCRIPTION

On the 3-string Dulcimer, only one string (String #1) is used for playing melodies.

On the 4-string Dulcimer, you have a double String #1 for the melody.

All strings are strummed in the "strum hollow" shown in preceding illustration. Strings 2 and 3 are harmonizing "drone" strings, the "drone" sound having somewhat of a bagpipe effect.

Chords are possible but very rarely used on the Dulcimer. Simple folk songs in the key of C, with no sharps or flats, may be sung with chords fretted with the fingers of the left hand, as follows:

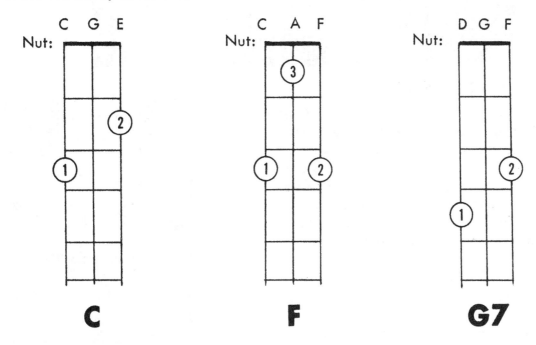

The Dulcimer has 12 or more diagonal lines across the fingerboard, separating the fingerboard into frets. Melodies are produced by pressing a so-called "Noter" in the various fret positions on String 1 (or on the double string 1 on the 4-string Dulcimer) to produce melodic tones. Some players do not use a noter. They prefer to simply press the string with the index finger or using all three center fingers of the left hand.

HOLDING THE INSTRUMENT

The player usually sits on a low stool or armless chair. The Dulcimer is placed flat across the knees, so that the tuning pegs are to the player's left (extending somewhat beyond the left knee). This way, the melody string (referred to as String 1) will be nearest you. You may want to tuck the right foot back beneath the chair to provide a level position.

The instrument should be slanted a little, so that the head is over your left knee, the other end pulled in toward your right hip.

THE NOTER

A finger-length wooden or bamboo bar (called a "Noter") is pressed on String 1 with your LEFT HAND. The clearest tone is obtained when you press the noter on the string(s) immediately to the left of the fret. Keep the end of the noter from touching the drone strings. It is held so that it covers only String 1 (the string nearest you). On the 4-string Dulcimer, String 1 is a double string.

Your thumb should be on top of the noter, pressing down.

The finger-tips are under the noter, with the index finger touching the fret board, so it may glide along the fingerboard on the melody string.

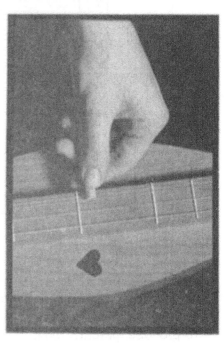

THE STRINGS

The string nearest the player is String 1 (a double string on the 4-String Dulcimer), called "E" String(s). String 2 is also an "E" String. The 3rd string is the "Bass String" or guitar "G" String. The strings are named for your convenience for replacement, if necessary, with guitar or (as some prefer) banjo strings.

THE FRETS

The frets on the Dulcimer govern the desired tones. They are separated by horizontal metal bars across the fingerboard. They are not numbered visibly. The first fret begins at the head near the sounding pegs. If you at first have difficulty in going from one fret to another, it is suggested you write in the fret numbers with chalk, erasable after you have advanced in playing and you know your frets instinctively.

STRUMMING

The strum (on the "strum hollow") provides the melody with a harmonizing chord which gives the Dulcimer its "drone" or bagpipe sound. The strum is accomplished in various ways.

A simple THUMB STRUM is used by many, as illustrated to the right. It has a sound per- haps more mellow than a pick, although a pick is preferred because of easier control.

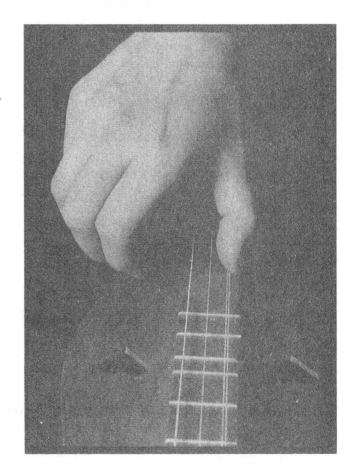

In fast tunes, with lots of notes, it is not necessary to strum all the strings with each note. The player may only pluck the melody string at times. The full strum need be used in these cases only at the beginning of a mea- sure or on each downbeat. On the other hand, as shown in some "rhythm songs" in this book, a player may effectively use more strums for the tune than there are melody notes.

As a rule, strumming consists of an inward picking toward yourself, so that the last tone of the strum is the melody string, which will sound more distinct than the drone strings.

After you strum this way, you can add a little spice to the tune by strumming inward (toward yourself) and away from yourself in between the melody notes to give a stronger beat to the song.

Sometimes, like in a jig or a polka, you can strum both towards and away from yourself with the melody to achieve the speed necessary for this type of song.

The more you play, the more you will want to experiment with various kinds of strumming.

THE PICK

There are many varieties of picks used for strumming with your right hand.

Goose and turkey quills, or any large feather shaved thin on the bottom end, and wooden picks, are all popular. Some prefer a small strip of leather. One of the picks commonly used is the little strip of celluloid which comes out of a man's shirt collar. You can doubtless obtain some sort of a pick where you bought your instrument, perhaps a light-weight guitar pick.

FINGER PICKING

The drone sound of the 2nd and 3rd strings will be sacrificed, but an agreeable tone can be derived from finger picking these strings.

Finger picking is usually done by the right hand middle and index fingers. For musical illustration and further direction, see page 87.

When playing this way, always try to pluck the melody slightly harder so that it will stand out from the accompaniment.

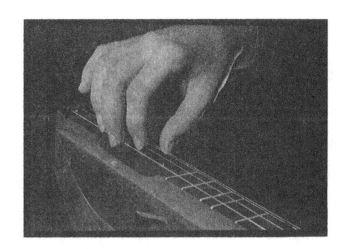

TUNING

The basic tuning for the Dulcimer is "MAJOR TUNING" (technically known as the "Ionian Mode").

The following section of the center of a piano keyboard shows the notes used if you are using a piano for tuning the Dulcimer:

Middle C

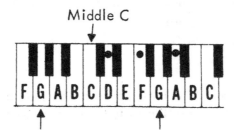

These instructions are primarily for the 3-String Dulcimer. In the 4-String Dulcimer, there are two melody strings (two #1 strings) producing a stronger melodic effect than a single string. In these instructions, you will consider them as one string.

String 1 is the melody string (nearest you) usually tuned to G (on piano keyboard, see above). String 2 is likewise usually tuned to G. String 3 (the "bass string") is usually tuned to C.

Apart from a piano, you may use a standard "pitch pipe" available in all music stores, which will give you the same basis for tuning. Or, as mentioned later, you may use "relative tuning".

First, we discuss tuning the Dulcimer to a piano, pitch-pipe or any other instrument you may choose. We start from String 3 (the "bass string") farthest from your body.

Play C note (per above diagram) on the keyboard, pitch-pipe or other instrument to which you are tuning. If a piano, hold your foot on the sustaining pedal, so that the note will ring clearly.

Now, pluck String 3 with the thumb of your right hand, in the "strum hollow" of the Dulcimer. It's an "open string", which means that no strings are pressed on the frets. Your left hand is on the String 3 tuning peg, for raising or lowering the pitch to match the sound of the C note.

Note. - The strings are supposed to be wound around the tuning pegs so that they are raised in pitch by turning clockwise and lowered in pitch by turning counter-clockwise. When replacing snapped strings, always start by turning the tuning peg clockwise.

The next step is to tune the 2nd string the same way as you did the 3rd string, but this time you will play the G note directly above the middle C for tuning.

Finally, you will tune the melody string(s) nearest you, using the same G note as you did for String 2.

To check the tuning, press the bass string on the 4th fret with the index finger of your left hand and pluck each string with your right thumb in the "strum hollow" and they should all have the same pitch. Your Dulcimer is now tuned "G - G - C".

But, the result may not be acceptable to your voice or you may not have another instrument with which to tune. Many singers prefer to sing in a lower key than the C tuning produces. In this event, you will use what we call "Relative Tuning", which means "tune to itself rather than to another instrument".

RELATIVE TUNING

In "relative tuning", you proceed as follows:

Start from String 3 (the "bass string") because Strings 1 and 2 are tuned in relationship to String 3. Find a reasonable tension on String 3 by turning the tuning peg, not too tightly or you may snap the string.

Press down with the index finger of your left hand on the 4th fret of String 3. Pluck string 3 with thumb of the right hand in the "strum hollow" and immediately pluck String 2. If String 2 is either higher or lower in pitch than String 3, turn the tuning peg with the right hand until String 2 matches. Your left hand remains on fret 4 of String 3.

Sometimes you have to go back and forth several times from "tuning peg" to "strum hollow" to produce the exact note on String 2.

Remove left hand from fret 4. String(s) 1 will be tuned without fretting.

String 1 has to match the pitch of String 2.

Pluck String 2 "open" (unfretted) in strum hollow with right hand, keeping left hand on tuning peg of String 1. Pluck String 1 immediately and turn tuning peg until String 1 matches String 2. Your Dulcimer is now in tune.

Try singing the well-known scale "do re mi fa sol la si do" along with the Dulcimer. The first note "do" falls at the 3rd fret on the melody String 1.

To play a scale, take the noter in your left hand and press on the 3rd fret. Pluck the melody string in the "strum hollow", advancing along the fingerboard, one fret at a time, playing a note for each fret. The 8th note (going from fret 3 to fret 10) completes the major scale.

A key preferred by many singers is the key of G. To establish the proper sounds (in harmony with a guitar, piano, etc.) it is suggested that you tune String 3 (the bass string) to G below middle C and the other strings to the D immediately to the right of C.

To check the tuning and pitch of the instrument, it is suggested that you try playing the first few bars of the melody of the familiar "Down In The Valley", using the fret numbers indicated:

The string sounded will correspond to the keyboard sound.

See keyboard on Page 8 if you need to find these piano notes

MINOR KEYS

Some songs are played in a minor key, and we have included several at the end of this book.

The minor scale is known as the "Aeolian Mode". The previously covered major scale is known as the "Ionian Mode". These are two of many modes in music scales, but these two modes cover just about every song.

To tune from the major (Ionian) to the minor (Aeolian) key:

Press down with index finger of left hand on String 3 (the "bass string") on the 6th fret. Sound the note with thumb or pick, with right hand, in the "strum hollow".

Immediately pluck String 1 to match the sound of String 3.

This is done with tuning peg, raising the pitch to the tone of String 3 (approximately half a turn).

Leave the 2nd and 3rd strings as they were in the major tuning.

IMPORTANT -- In the minor tuning, the scale begins at the FIRST FRET and concludes on the EIGHTH FRET.

PRACTICAL APPLICATION

The songs in this book are presented in four horizontal units:

Unit 1 - top: Chord names for instruments which may accompany the Dulcimer
Unit 2 - below the chord names: Fret numbers to be pressed by left hand or "0"
                                   for "Open Strings", strummed but not pressed.
Unit 3 - Music notes for the songs. For those who do not read music at all, the
                                   fundamental principles inside the cover may be
                                   useful.
Unit 4 - Lyrics to the songs. This line does not exist in strictly instrumental pieces.

All "major key" songs in this book are written in the key of C, which has no sharps or flats in its scale.

All "minor key" songs are written in the key of C Minor, necessitating a different numbering system, as you will note in the songs comprising the minor key section of the book.

If you use "relative tuning" and you aren't actually in the key of C, you read the music the same as if you were in that key, because the fret numbers indicated will apply to whatever key you have tuned the instrument.

All melodies in this book are derived from the simple scale of "do re mi fa sol la si do", so you simply follow the fret numbers or, if you read music, the music notes.

Before playing the songs, it is advisable to get the sound and the feel of a simple major scale.

THE MAJOR SCALE

To play the major scale on the melody string, press the noter on the 3rd fret with left hand.

With your right hand thumb or pick, pluck the string in the "strum hollow". This is the first "do" of the scale.

The second note "re" is produced the same way, but the noter is pressed on the 4th fret.

Move one fret at a time, from left to right, to complete the scale at the 10th fret. This is the high "do".

You may find the diagram of frets and corresponding music notes, on the following page, a useful guide to the fret board.

DIAGRAM OF FRETS AND CORRESPONDING NOTES

NOTE. - The Figure 0 represents a tone which is picked or included in a strum, but not pressed by the noter.   This is known as an "open string".

**NUMBER SYSTEM FOR
MAJOR AND MINOR TUNING**

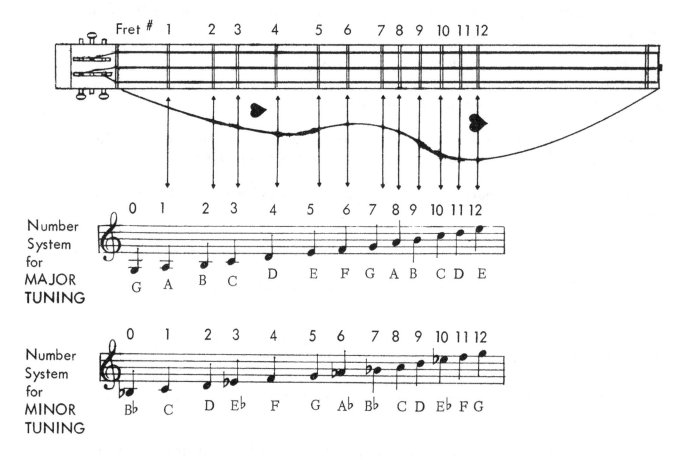

FIRST SONG

The number above each note shows the fret to be "Noted". The letters are chord names for pianists, guitarists, etc., to accompany the Dulcimer player with chords.

Chord names govern the tune, as it progresses, until a new chord is named.

REMEMBER! Place the noter over the melody string nearest you, but in such manner that it does not touch the adjacent strings, which will be strummed for the "drone" sound.

The first note in "Aunt Rhody" starts with the 5th fret, the "mi" in "do re mi".

Note. - All songs in this book are presented in the major key of C, except for a group of minor songs included in the final section of the book.

AUNT RHODY

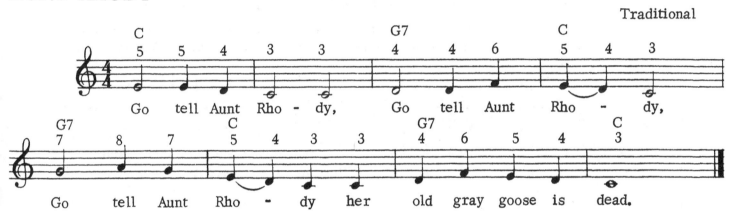

Go tell Aunt Rho - dy, Go tell Aunt Rho - dy,

Go tell Aunt Rho - dy her old gray goose is dead.

BROTHER JOHN

(Frere Jacques)
French Song

Are you sleep-ing? Are you sleep-ing? Broth-er John, Broth-er John,

Morn-ing bells are ring-ing, Morn-ing bells are ring-ing, Ding ding dong! Ding ding dong!

* 0 is a tone picked or included in a strum, but not pressed by noter. It is known as an "open string".

LONDON BRIDGE

MARY HAD A LITTLE LAMB

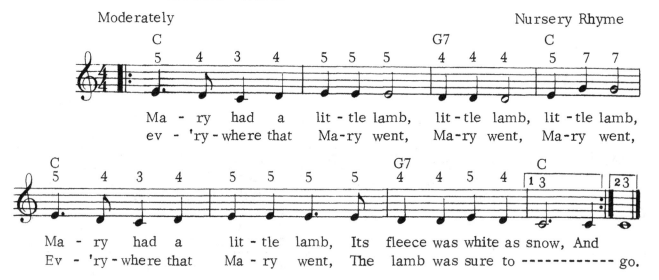

TEN LITTLE INDIANS

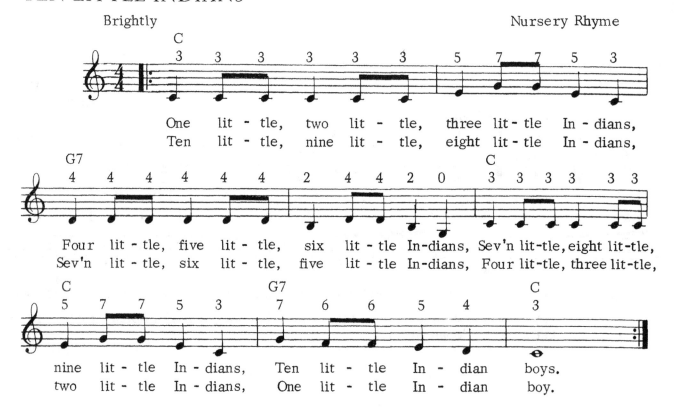

THREE BLIND MICE

Nursery Rhyme

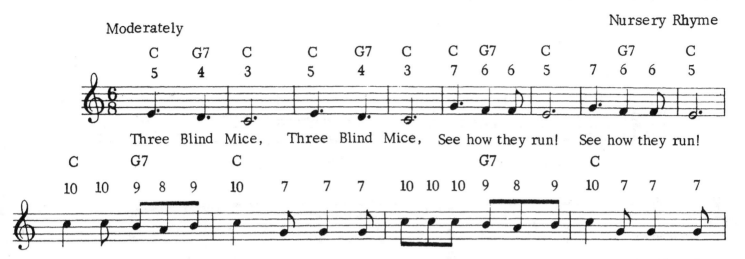

Three Blind Mice, Three Blind Mice, See how they run! See how they run!

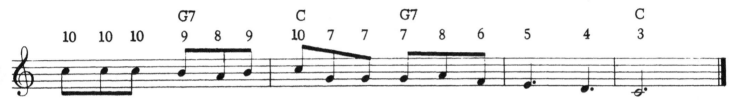

They ran af - ter the farm - er's wife, She cried to the farm-er: "Oh save my life!" The

farm - er said: "Don't be a - fraid of the nice lit - tle Three Blind Mice."

SING A SONG OF SIXPENCE

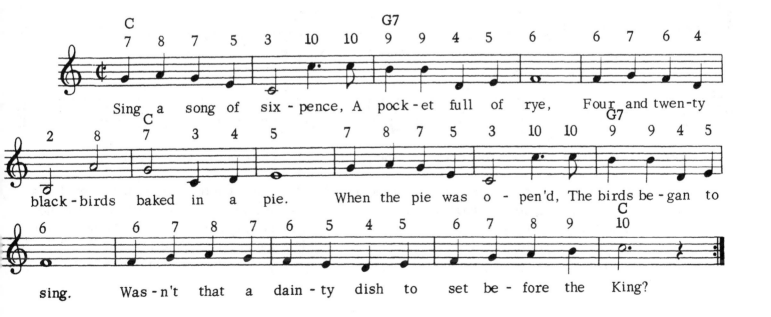

Sing a song of six - pence, A pock - et full of rye, Four and twen-ty

black - birds baked in a pie. When the pie was o - pen'd, The birds be - gan to

sing. Was - n't that a dain - ty dish to set be - fore the King?

16

ROW, ROW, ROW YOUR BOAT

Row, row, row your boat, Gent - ly down the stream,

Mer-ri - ly, mer-ri - ly, mer - ri - ly, mer - ri - ly, Life is but a dream.

* In single-tone triplets, it is optional to play the tone once or 3 times to the count, as you wish.

DOWN IN THE VALLEY

Moderately   Traditional

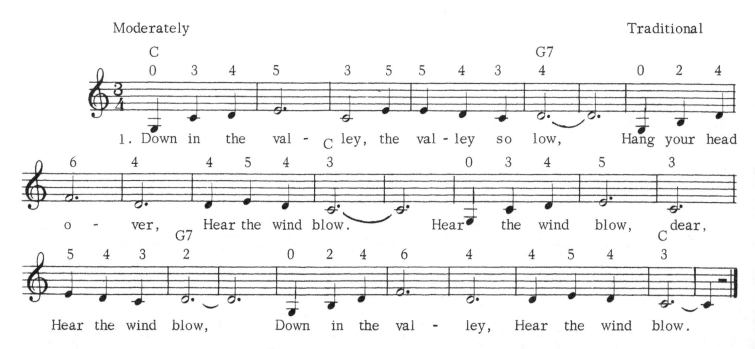

1. Down in the val - ley, the val - ley so low, Hang your head

o - ver, Hear the wind blow. Hear the wind blow, dear,

Hear the wind blow, Down in the val - ley, Hear the wind blow.

2. Give my heart ease, dear, Oh give my heart ease,
Think of me, darling, give my heart ease.
Write me a letter, send it by mail,
Send it in care of - Birmingham Jail.
  (Repeat #1)

3. Write me a letter, with just a few lines,
Answer me, darling, will you be mine?
I make a promise to go straight and true,
I'll spend a life-time just loving you.
  (Repeat #1)

THIS OLD MAN

Lively

Traditional

This old man, He plays *"one", He plays knick-knack on his drum, With a knick knack pad-dy wack, Give a dog a bone, This old man came roll - ing home.

* Two - He plays knick knack on a shoe, etc.
Three - "on the tree" &c   Four - "on the door" &c
Five - "on the hive" &c   Six - "on the sticks" &c
Seven - He plays knick knack up in Heaven, &c
Eight - "on the gate" &c   Nine - "on the line" &c
Ten - He plays knick knack once again, etc.

LONG, LONG AGO

Moderately

THOMAS BAYLY

Tell me the tales that to me were so dear, Long long a - go, Long long a - go. Sing me the songs I de - light - ed to hear, Long long a - go, long a - go. Now you are here, all my grief is re - moved, Let me for - get that so long you have rov'd. Let me be - lieve that you love as you loved, Long long a - go, long a - go.

BIRTHDAY THEME

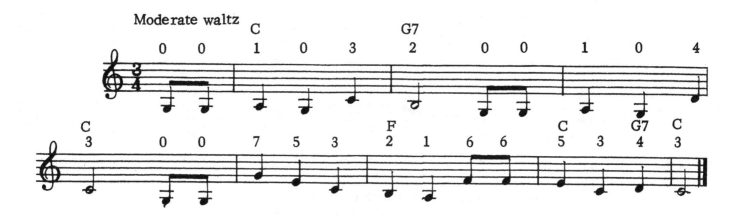

BLOW THE MAN DOWN

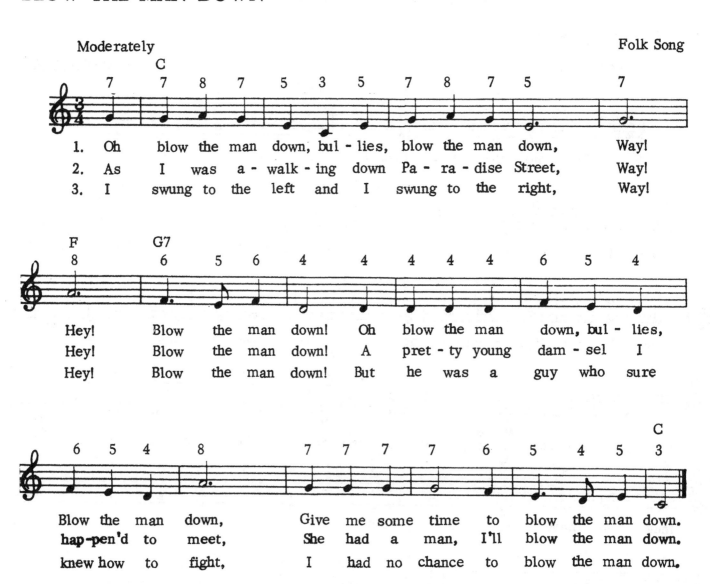

1. Oh blow the man down, bul - lies, blow the man down, Way!
2. As I was a - walk - ing down Pa - ra - dise Street, Way!
3. I swung to the left and I swung to the right, Way!

Hey! Blow the man down! Oh blow the man down, bul - lies,
Hey! Blow the man down! A pret - ty young dam - sel I
Hey! Blow the man down! But he was a guy who sure

Blow the man down, Give me some time to blow the man down.
hap-pen'd to meet, She had a man, I'll blow the man down.
knew how to fight, I had no chance to blow the man down.

MY DARLING CLEMENTINE

Moderately   Folk Song

1. In a cav - ern, In a can - yon, Ex-ca - vat - ing for a
2. Oh my dar - ling, Oh my dar - ling, Oh my dar - ling Clem-en-

mine, Dwelt a min - er, For-ty nin - er, And his daugh-ter, Clem-en -tine.
tine, You are lost and gone for - ev - er, Dread-ful sor - ry, Clem-en - tine.

3. She drove ducklings to the water
Ev'ry morning just at nine,
Hit her big toe 'gainst a splinter,
Fell into the foaming brine.

(Repeat #2)

4. Ruby lips above the water,
Blowing bubbles soft and fine,
But, alas, I was no swimmer,
So I lost my Clementine.

(Repeat #2)

CARELESS LOVE

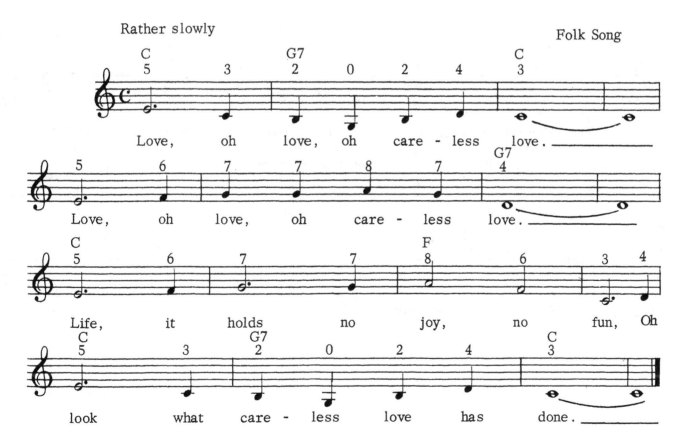

Rather slowly   Folk Song

Love, oh love, oh care - less love. _____

Love, oh love, oh care - less love. _____

Life, it holds no joy, no fun, Oh

look what care - less love has done. _____

AMERICA

Text by
Rev. Samuel Smith

Moderately

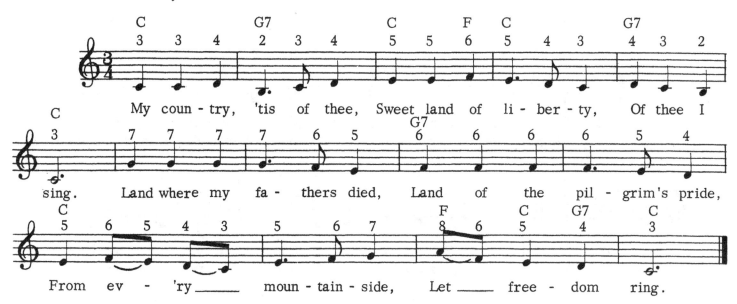

My coun - try, 'tis of thee, Sweet land of li - ber - ty, Of thee I sing. Land where my fa - thers died, Land of the pil - grim's pride, From ev - 'ry_____ moun - tain - side, Let _____ free - dom ring.

SHENANDOAH

Folk Song

Oh Shen - an - doah, __ I long to hear you, A - way, __ you roll - ing riv - er, _____ Oh Shen - an - doah, __ I long to hear you, A - way, _____ We're bound a - way, 'Cross the wide Mis - sou - ri.

THE CAISSONS GO ROLLING ALONG

U.S. FIELD ARTILLERY SONG

MARINES' HYMN

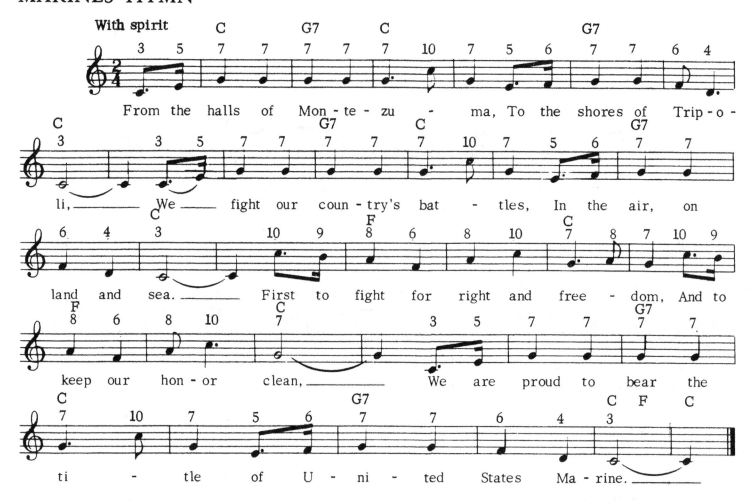

THE CRUEL WAR IS RAGING

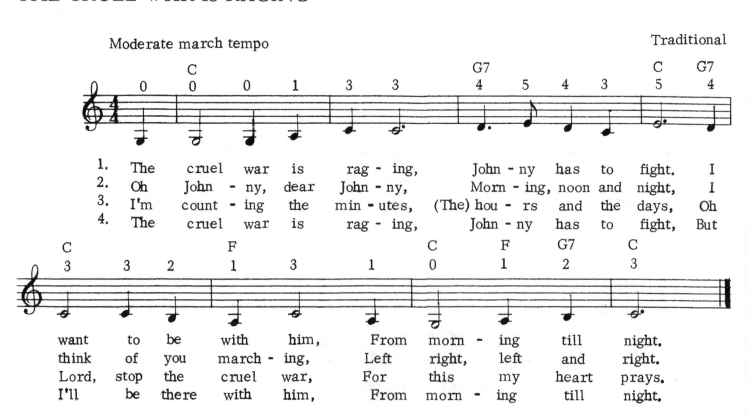

THE BATTLE HYMN OF THE REPUBLIC

STEFFE & HOWE

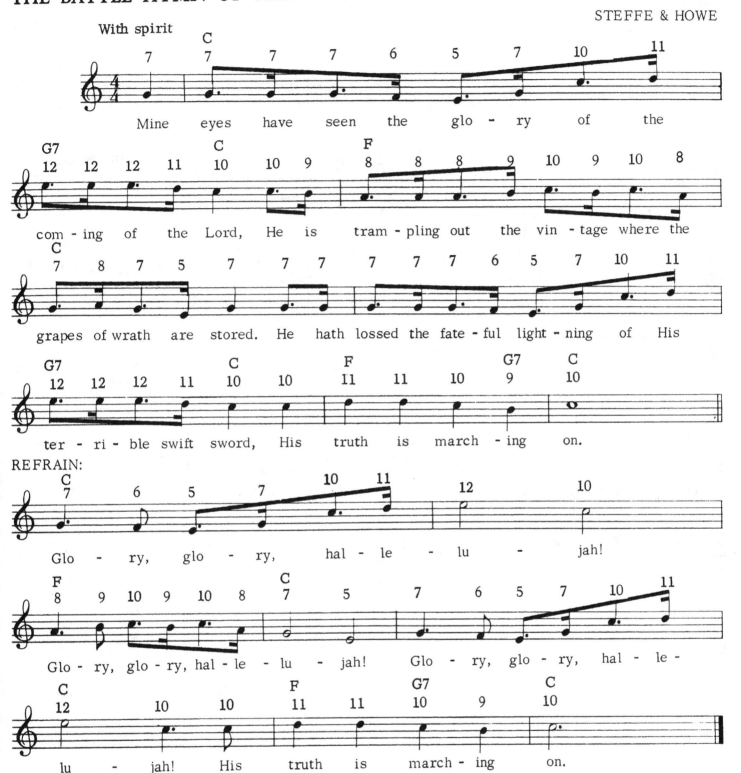

2. I have seen Him in the watch-fires of a hundred circling camps,
They have build-ed Him an altar in the evening dews and damps.
I can read His righteous sentence by the dim and flaring lamps,
His day is marching on. (Repeat Refrain)

3. He has sounded forth the trumpet that shall never call retreat,
He is sifting out the hearts of men before His judgment seat.
Oh, be swift, my soul, to answer Him! Be jubilant, my feet!
Our God is marching on. (Repeat Refrain)

DIXIE

With spirit

DANIEL D. EMMETT

RED RIVER VALLEY

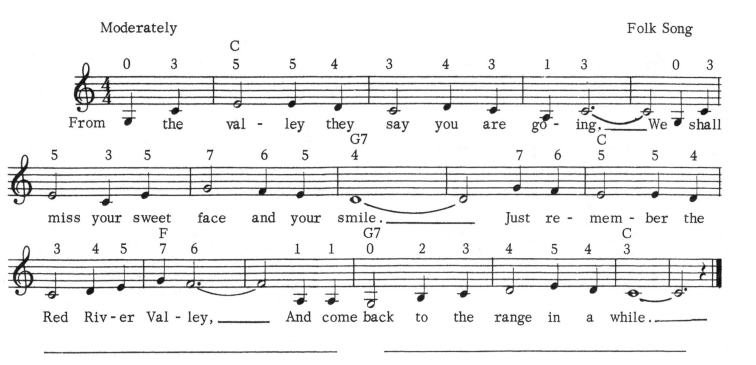

WILDWOOD FLOWER

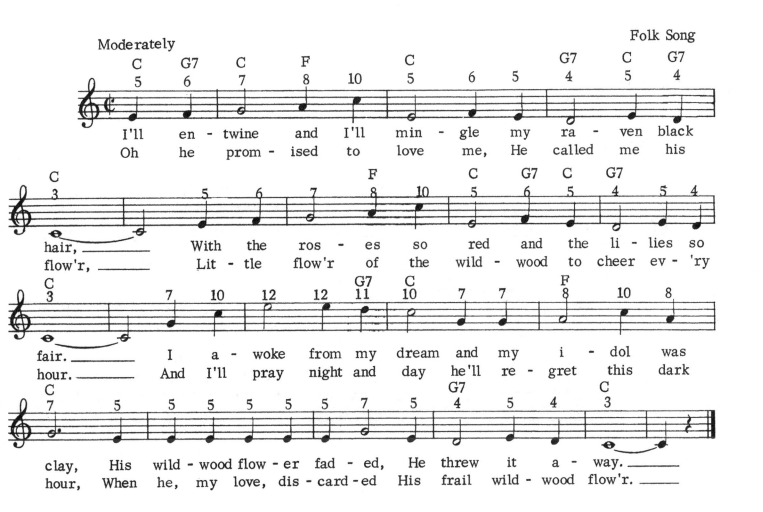

MY BONNIE

Scottish Folk Song

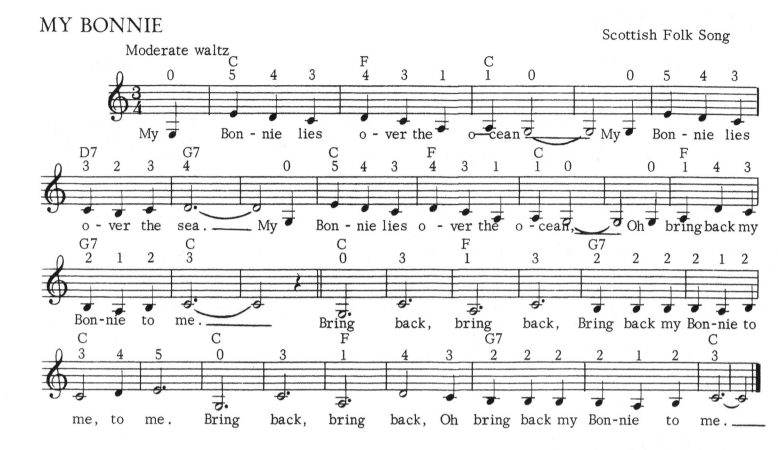

THE CAN CAN

JACQUES OFFENBACH

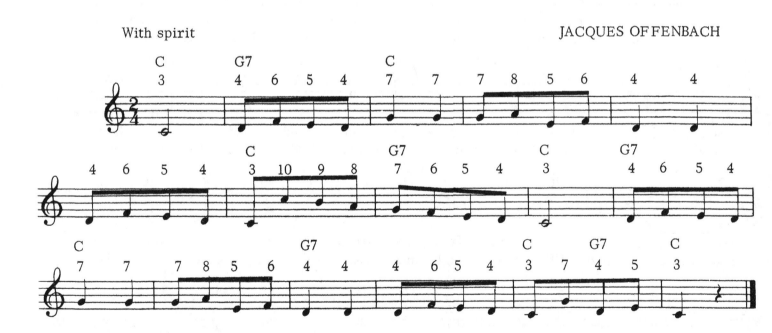

HOME, SWEET HOME

Words by JOHN H. PAYNE
Music by HENRY R. BISHOP

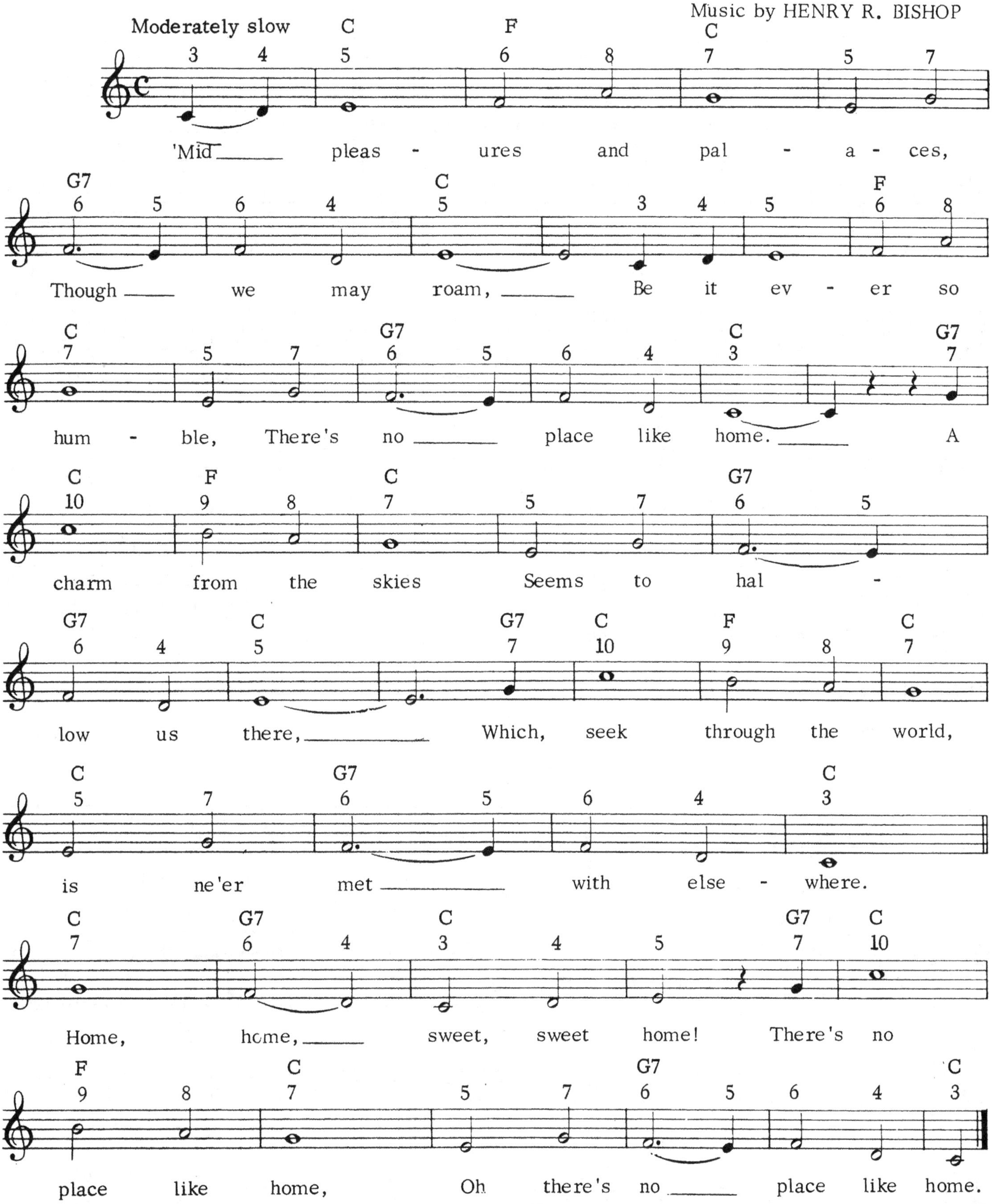

WHEN THE SAINTS GO MARCHING IN

DEEP RIVER

AMAZING GRACE

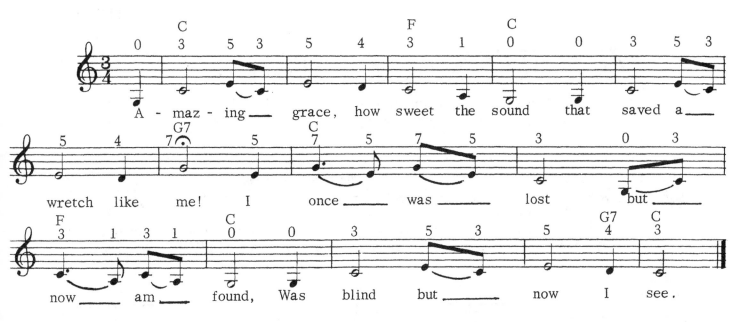

HAND ME DOWN MY WALKING CANE

HE'S GOT THE WHOLE WORLD IN HIS HANDS

NEARER, MY GOD, TO THEE

NEWMAN & DYKES

GIVE ME THAT OLD TIME RELIGION

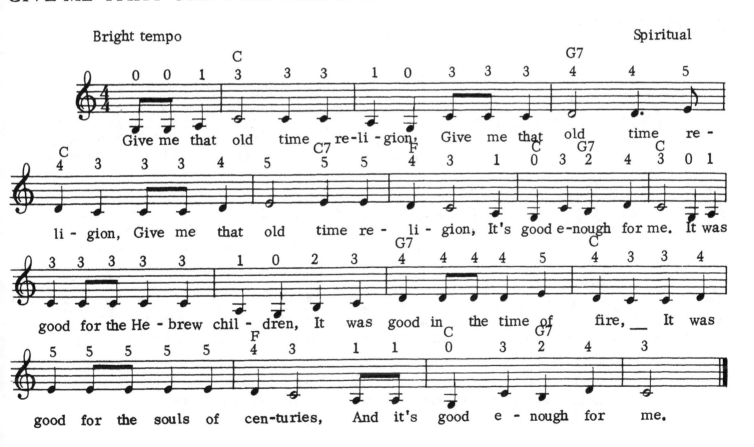

GO TELL IT ON THE MOUNTAIN

SPIRITUAL

Go tell it on the moun - tain, O - ver the hills and ev - 'ry-where,

Go tell it on the moun - tain, I saw my Lord stand-ing there. Oh there.

1 When I was a sin - ner, I prayed both night and day, I
2 When I was a seek - er, I sought both night and day, I

asked the Lord to help me, And He showed me the way. Oh
asked the Lord to help me, And He taught me to ------------------- pray.

(Repeat A to Fine)

ROCK OF AGES

Slowly

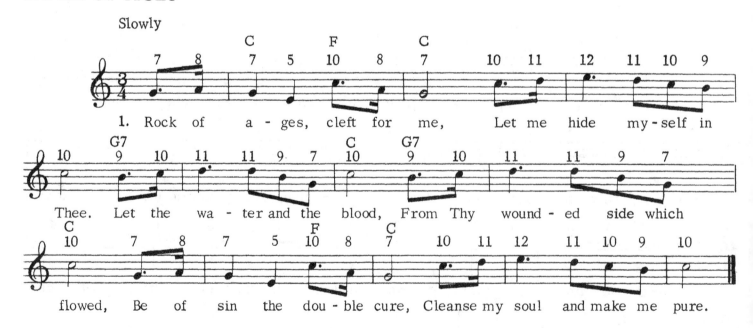

1. Rock of a - ges, cleft for me, Let me hide my - self in

Thee. Let the wa - ter and the blood, From Thy wound - ed side which

flowed, Be of sin the dou - ble cure, Cleanse my soul and make me pure.

2. While I draw this fleeting breath, till my eyelids close in death,
   When I soar to worlds unknown, and behold Thee on Thy throne,
   Rock of ages, cleft for me, Let me hide myself in Thee!

LEAD KINDLY LIGHT

BAKER & DYKES

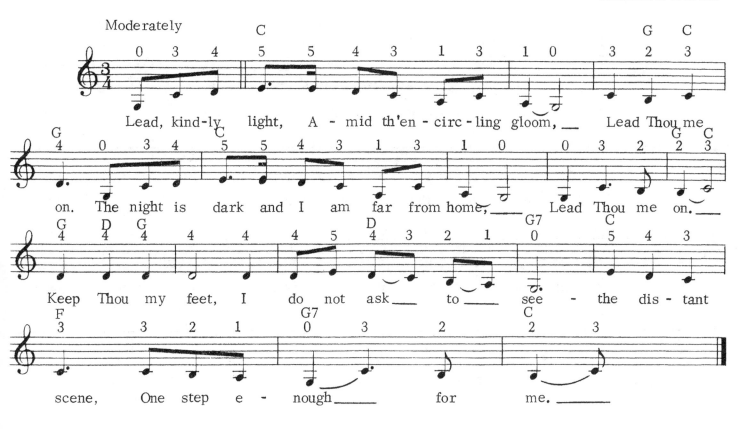

GOD BE WITH YOU TILL WE MEET AGAIN

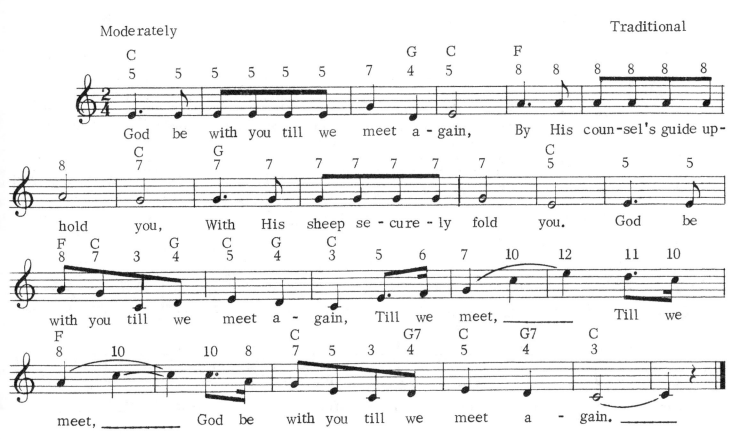

NOBODY KNOWS THE TROUBLE I'VE SEEN

WERE YOU THERE?

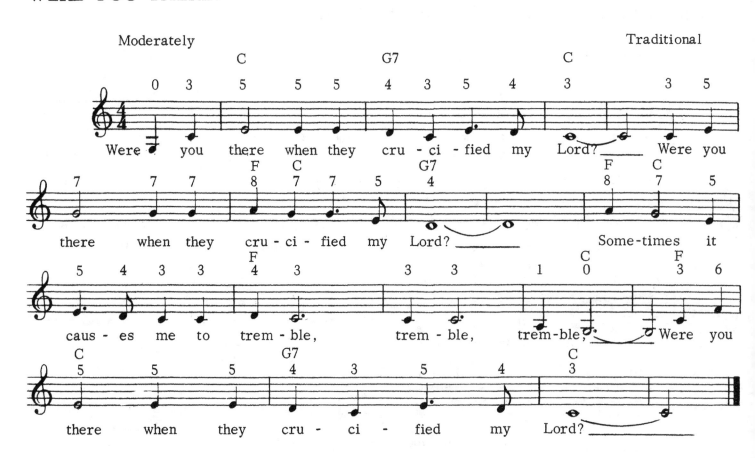

OH HAPPY DAY

DODDRIDGE and RIMBAULT

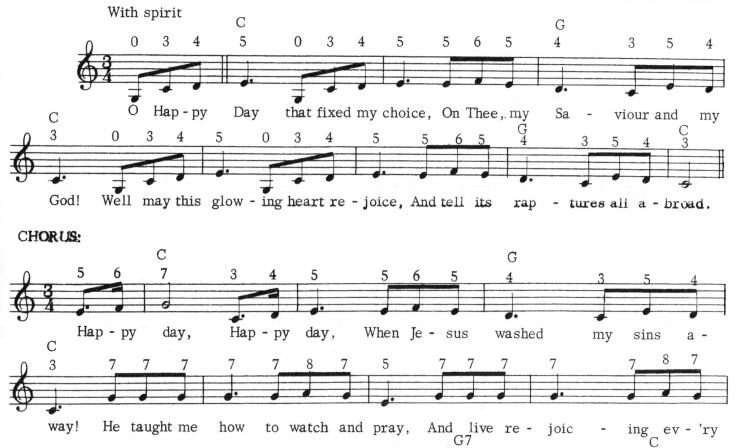

COUNT YOUR BLESSINGS

OATMAN and EXCELL

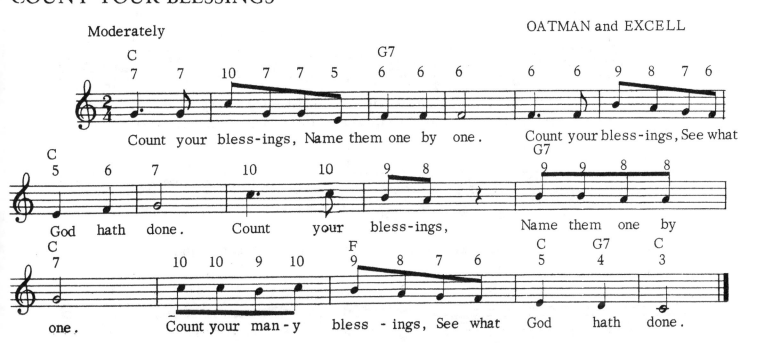

SONG OF JOY

LUDWIG VAN BEETHOVEN
(From Symphony #9)

Sing! Sing a Song Of Joy, The joy of love and broth-er-hood.

Sing! Sing a Song Of Joy, The joy of peace, when life is good.

Joy comes to me and to you when-ev-er we do each oth-er good,

So sing a Song Of Joy, To peace, to love, to broth-er-hood.

NELLY WAS A LADY

STEPHEN FOSTER

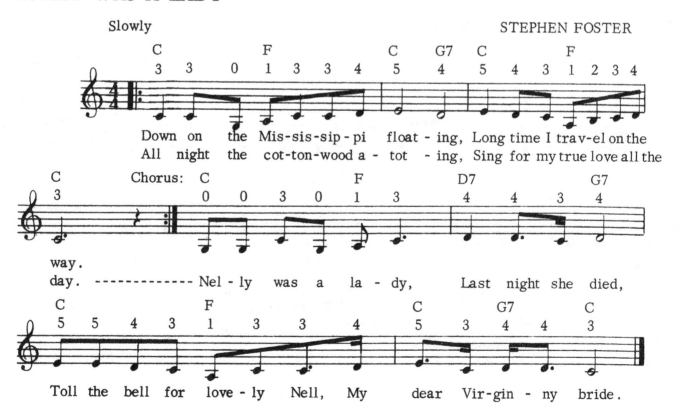

Down on the Mis-sis-sip-pi float-ing, Long time I trav-el on the
All night the cot-ton-wood a-tot-ing, Sing for my true love all the

way.
day. ------------- Nel-ly was a lady, Last night she died,

Toll the bell for love-ly Nell, My dear Vir-gin-ny bride.

SWING LOW, SWEET CHARIOT

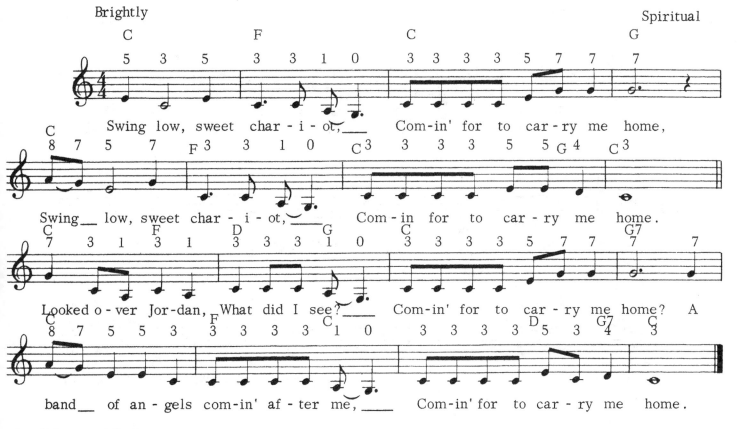

JACOB'S LADDER

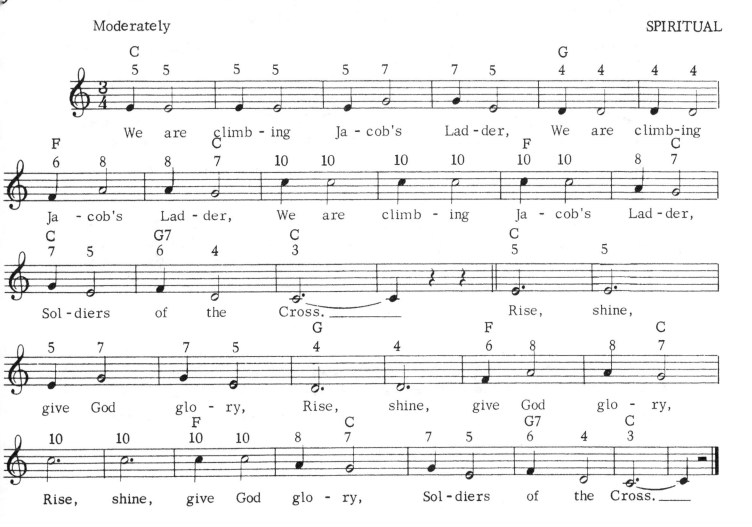

JINGLE BELLS

Brightly

Christmas Song

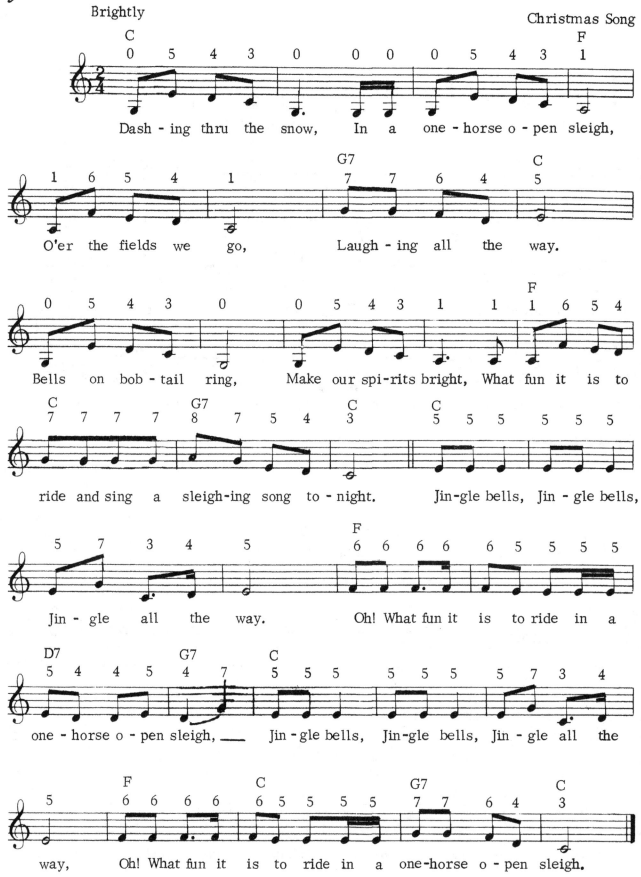

SILENT NIGHT

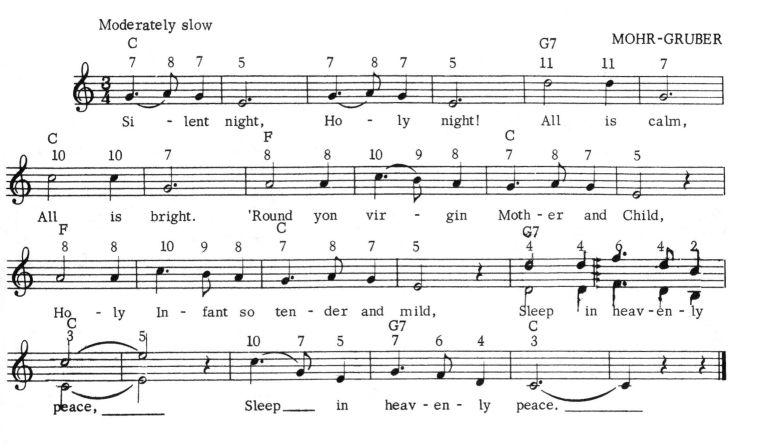

O COME, ALL YE FAITHFUL

GOOD KING WENCESLAS

Moderately

Christmas Song

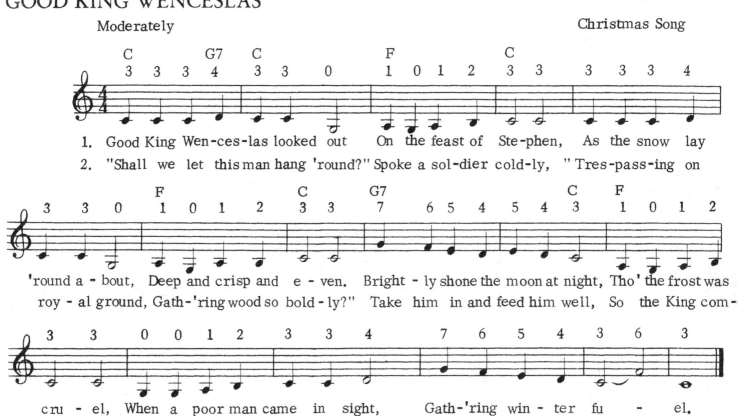

1. Good King Wen-ces-las looked out On the feast of Ste-phen, As the snow lay
2. "Shall we let this man hang 'round?" Spoke a sol-dier cold-ly, "Tres-pass-ing on

'round a - bout, Deep and crisp and e - ven. Bright - ly shone the moon at night, Tho' the frost was
roy - al ground, Gath-'ring wood so bold - ly?" Take him in and feed him well, So the King com-

cru - el, When a poor man came in sight, Gath-'ring win - ter fu - el.
mand - ed, Hear ye now the Christ-mas bell, Try to un - der stand __ it.

O CHRISTMAS TREE

Moderately

Christmas Song

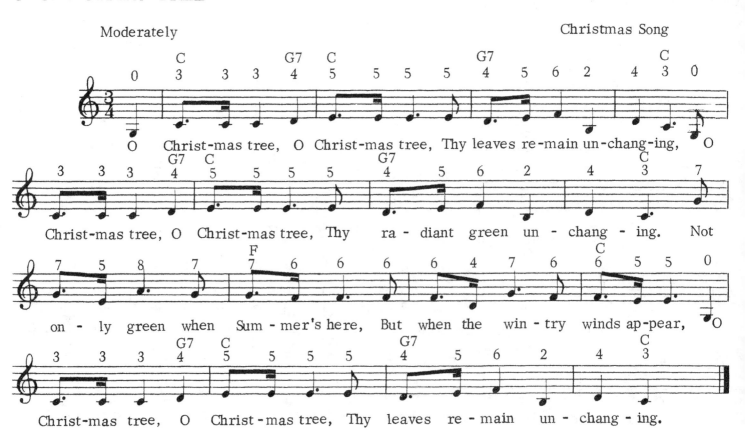

O Christ-mas tree, O Christ-mas tree, Thy leaves re-main un-chang-ing, O

Christ-mas tree, O Christ-mas tree, Thy ra - diant green un - chang - ing. Not

on - ly green when Sum - mer's here, But when the win - try winds ap-pear, O

Christ-mas tree, O Christ-mas tree, Thy leaves re - main un - chang - ing.

THE FIRST NOEL

Christmas Song

WE WISH YOU A MERRY CHRISTMAS

Christmas Song

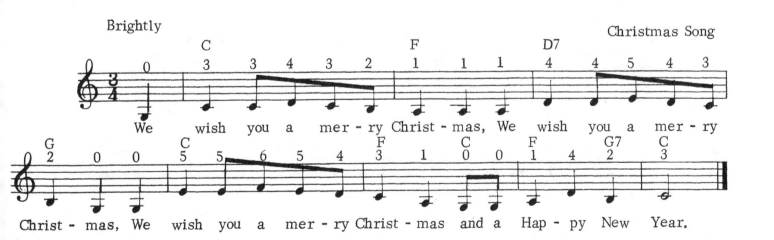

FRANKIE AND JOHNNY

Moderately slow

Traditional

1. Frank-ie and John - ny were lov - ers, Oh Lord - y, how__ they could love. They swore to be true__ to each oth - er, True as the stars a - bove, He was her man, _____ But he done her wrong.__

2. Frankie went down to the hotel,
Looked in the window so high,
There she saw her lovin' Johnny -
Make love to Alice Bly,
He was her man but he done her wrong.

3. Johnny saw Frankie a-comin',
Down the back stairs he did scoot,
Frankie - she took out her pistol,
Boy! How that gal could shoot,
He was her man but he done her wrong.

4. Frankie, she said to the warden,
What are they going to do?
Warden replied, sorry Frankie,
It's the 'lectric chair for you,
You shot your man tho' he did you wrong.

5. Frankie, she went to the big chair,
Calm as a lady could be,
Turning her eyes up, she whisper'd -
Lord, I'm coming up to Thee,
He was my man, but he done me wrong.

SKIP TO MY LOU

Lively

Folk Song

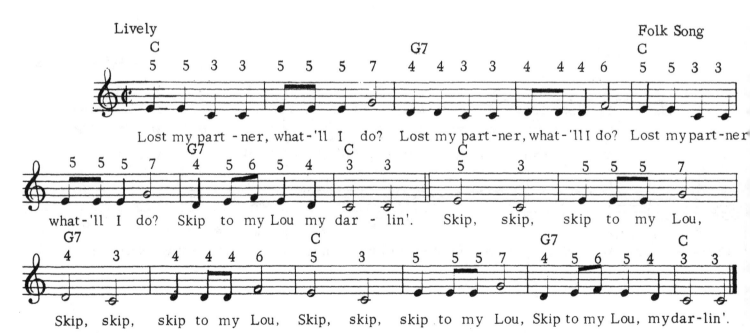

Lost my part - ner, what -'ll I do? Lost my part-ner, what-'ll I do? Lost my part-ner what-'ll I do? Skip to my Lou my dar - lin'. Skip, skip, skip to my Lou,

Skip, skip, skip to my Lou, Skip, skip, skip to my Lou, Skip to my Lou, my dar-lin'.

THE BOWERY

THE BLUE TAIL FLY

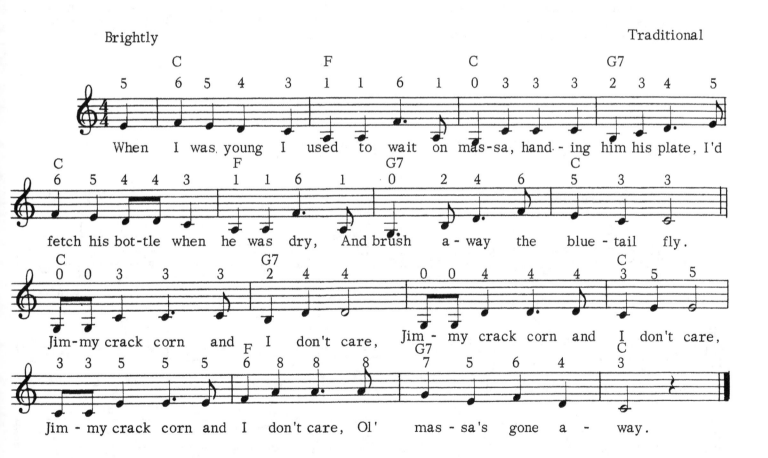

THE STREETS OF LAREDO

Cowboy song

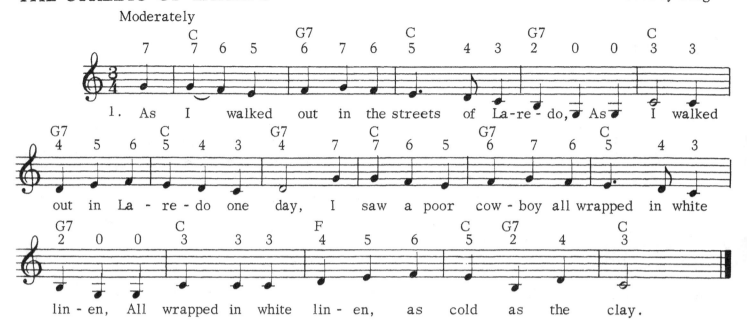

2. "I see by your outfit that you are a cowboy,"
   These words he did say as I boldly stepped by;
   "Come sit down beside me and hear my sad story;
   I was shot in the breast and I know I must die."

3. "It was once in the saddle I used to go dashing,
   It was once in the saddle I used to be gay;
   First to the dram-house and then to the card-house;
   Got shot in the breast and I'm dying today.

4. "Go fetch me some water, a cup of cold water
   To cool my parched lips," the poor cowboy said;
   Before I returned, his spirit had left him,
   No one could revive him; the cowboy was dead.

5. We carried him out to a lovely green valley,
   And there dug a grave by the afternoon light;
   And now when I walk on the streets of Laredo
   I think of the cowboy in linen so white.

OH BURY ME NOT ON THE LONE PRAIRIE

GOOD-BYE, OLD PAINT

Moderately

Cowboy Song

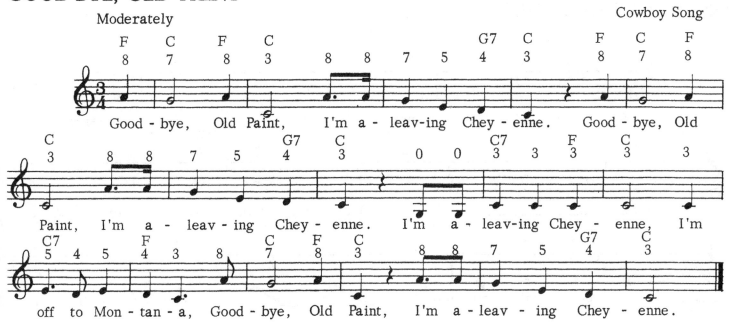

Good - bye, Old Paint, I'm a - leav-ing Chey - enne. Good - bye, Old Paint, I'm a - leav - ing Chey - enne. I'm a - leav-ing Chey - enne, I'm off to Mon - tan - a, Good - bye, Old Paint, I'm a - leav - ing Chey - enne.

TOM DOOLEY

Moderately

Appalachian Folk Song

Met her on the moun - tain, Swore she would be my wife, But the gal re - fused me, And so I took her life. Hang down your head, Tom Doo - ley, Hang down your head and cry, Hang down your head, Tom Doo-ley, Poor boy, you're gon-na die.

ON TOP OF OLD SMOKY

Folk Song

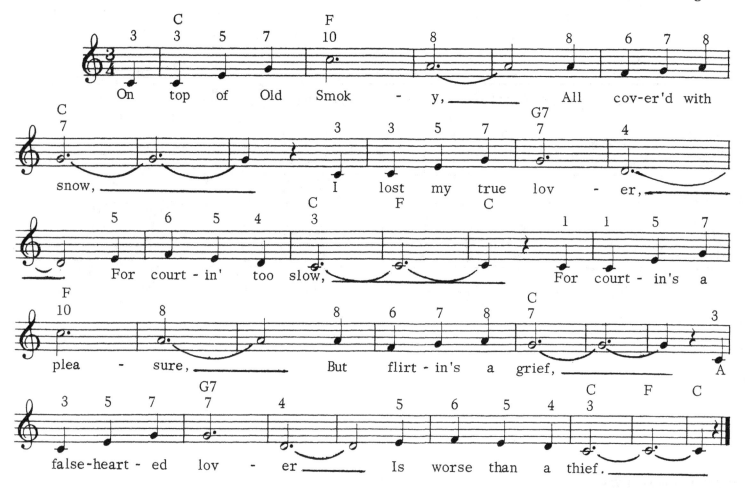

LOCH LOMOND

Scottish Song

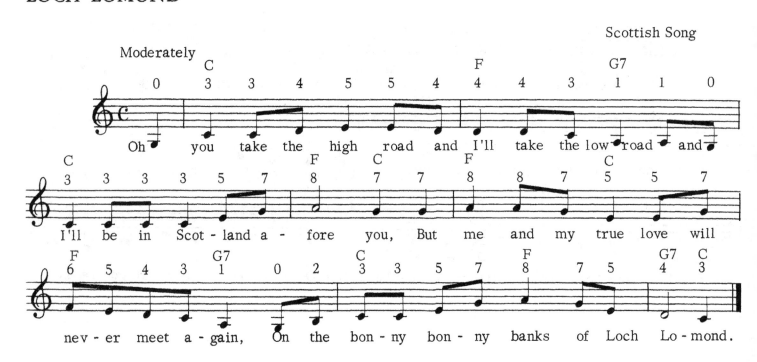

AURA LEE

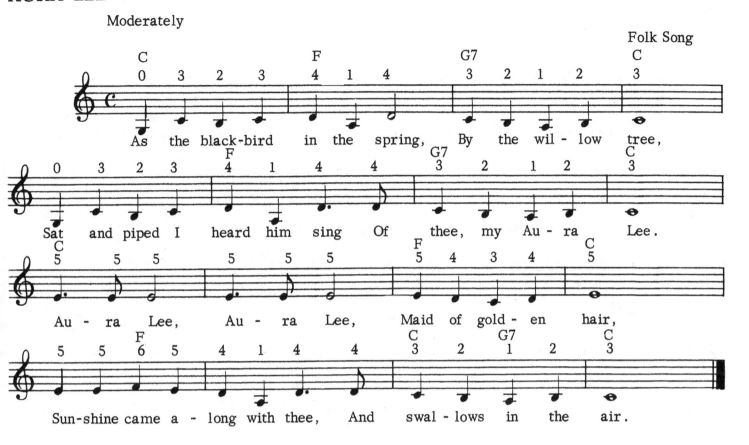

Moderately

Folk Song

As the black-bird in the spring, By the wil - low tree,

Sat and piped I heard him sing Of thee, my Au - ra Lee.

Au - ra Lee, Au - ra Lee, Maid of gold - en hair,

Sun-shine came a - long with thee, And swal - lows in the air.

JOHN HENRY

Slowly

Folk Song

1. John — Hen - ry said — to the cap - tain, "A —

man ain't noth-ing but a man, And be - fore I'll let your steam drill beat me down,

Die — with the ham-mer in my hand, O Lord! Die — with the ham-mer in my hand!

2. John Henry got a thirty pound hammer,
Beside the steam drill he did stand,
He beat that steam drill three inches down,
And died with his hammer in his hand, O Lord!
Died with the hammer in his hand.

3. John Henry had a handsome little son,
Sittin' in the palm of his hand,
He hugged and kissed him and bid him farewell,
Saying "Son, always do the best you can, O Lord!
Always do the best you can."

4. John Henry went straight to the graveyard,
And they buried him in the sand,
And ev'ry locomotive come roarin' by—
There lays a steel-drivin' man, O Lord!
There lays a steel-drivin' man.

BEAUTIFUL ISLE OF SOMEWHERE

THIS TRAIN

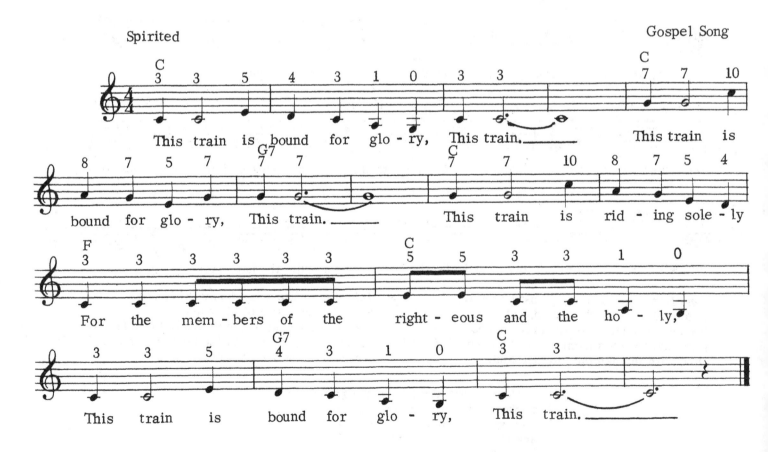

THE WABASH CANNONBALL

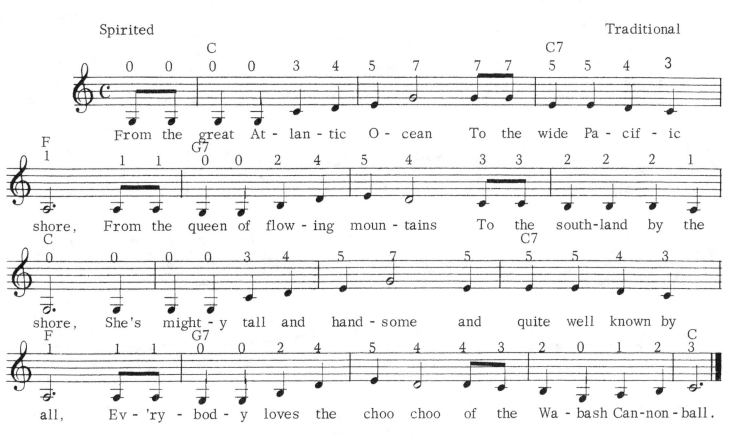

WORRIED MAN BLUES

COUNTRY GARDENS

Brightly

English Dance

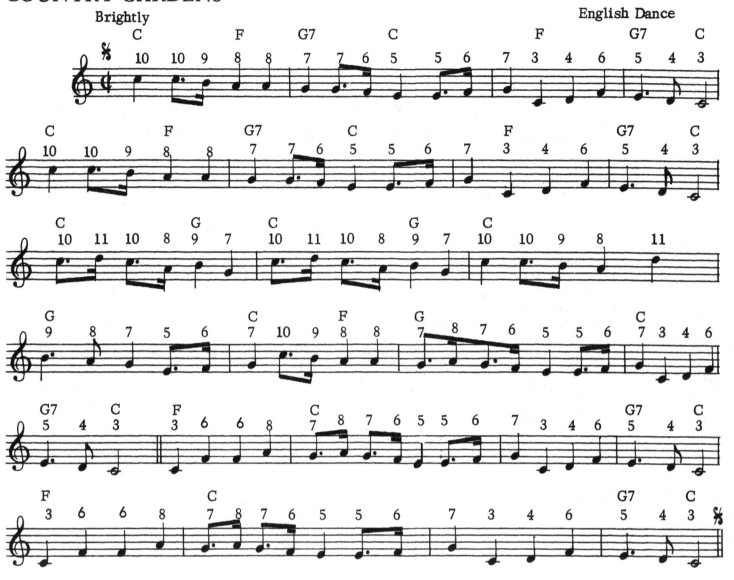

JULIDA POLKA

Brightly

Polish Polka

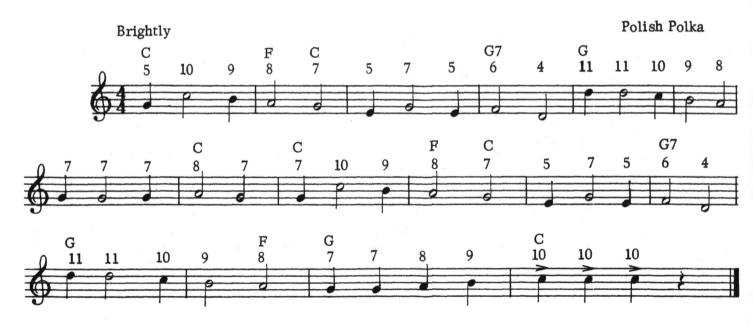

LULLABY

JOHANNES BRAHMS

LARGO (From "New World Symphony")

ANTON DVORAK

MARY ANN

Folk Song of Trinidad
Adaptation by BERNARD GASSO

Brightly

GUANTANAMERA

Moderately

MARTI and GASSO

Guan-ta-na-mer-a, gua-ji-ra Guan-ta-na-mer-a.

Guan-ta-na-mer - a, gua-ji-ra Guan-ta-na-mer-a.

Verse:

I'm just a man who is try-ing To do some good be-fore dy-ing,

To ask each man and his broth-er To bear no ill tow'rd each

oth-er. This life will nev-er be hol - low To those who lis-ten and fol - low.

(D. S. al Fine)

LA CUCARACHA

Brightly

Cuban Folk Song

La Cu-ca-ra-cha,— La Cu-ca-ra-cha,— Yo no pue-de ca-mi-

nar,— Por que no tien - e,— Por que le fal - ta —— Ci-ga-ril-los que fu-mar.

DRINK TO ME ONLY WITH THINE EYES

Old English

VILIA

FRANZ LEHAR

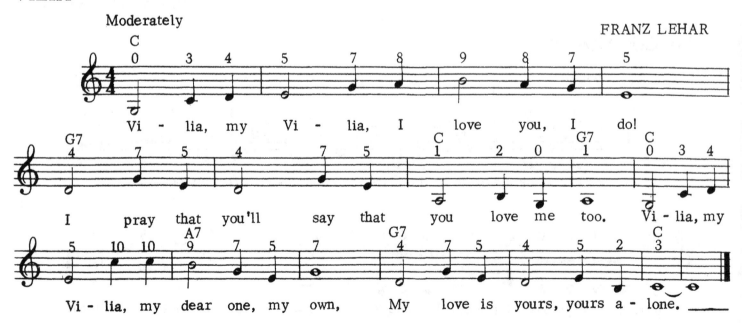

HOME ON THE RANGE

BUFFALO GALS

Brightly

Folk Song

As I was walk-ing down the street, down the street, down the street, A sweet lit-tle girl I chanced to meet, She was fair to see. Oh! Buf-fa-lo gals, won't you come out to-night? Come out to-night! Come out to-night! Buf-fa-lo gals, won't you come out to-night, And Dance By The Light Of The Moon?

I'VE BEEN WORKING ON THE RAILROAD

Moderately

Traditional

I've been work-ing on the rail-road, All the live-long day. I've been work-ing on the rail-road, To pass the time a-way. Don't you hear the whis-tle blow-ing? Rise up ear-ly in the morn. Don't you hear the Cap-tain shout-ing: "Oh Di-nah, blow your horn!"

THAT'S WHERE MY MONEY GOES

That's where my mon-ey goes,___ To buy my ba-by clothes,___
That's where my mon-ey goes,___ Tak-ing her out to shows,___

I buy her ev-ry-thing from head to her toes.
Love can be quite ex-pen-sive, This lov-er knows.

I'm hers un-til the end,___ On her I love to spend,___
Oh but my heart will sing___ When she ac-cepts my ring,___

Say boys, that's where my mon-ey goes.___
Say boys, that's where my mon-ey goes.___

I WISH I WAS SINGLE AGAIN

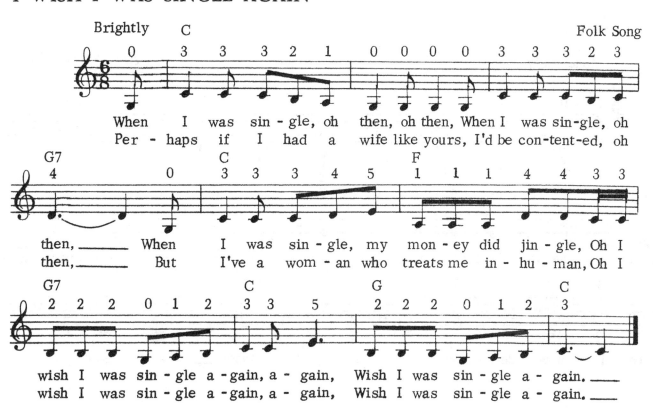

When I was sin-gle, oh then, oh then, When I was sin-gle, oh
Per-haps if I had a wife like yours, I'd be con-tent-ed, oh

then,___ When I was sin-gle, my mon-ey did jin-gle, Oh I
then,___ But I've a wom-an who treats me in-hu-man, Oh I

wish I was sin-gle a-gain, a-gain, Wish I was sin-gle a-gain.___
wish I was sin-gle a-gain, a-gain, Wish I was sin-gle a-gain.___

SWEET ROSIE O'GRADY
Moderate waltz

MAUDE NUGENT

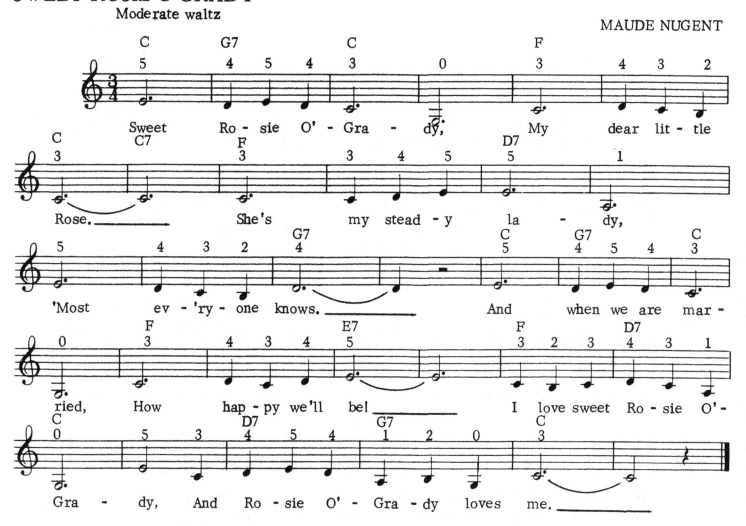

ALOHA OE

Moderately

QUEEN LILIUOKALANI

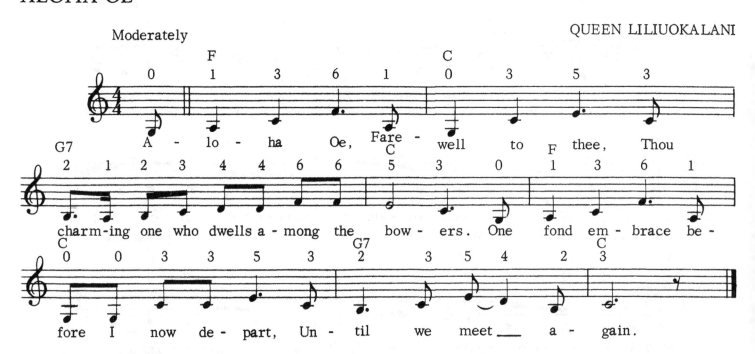

COMIN' THRU THE RYE

Moderately

Folk Song

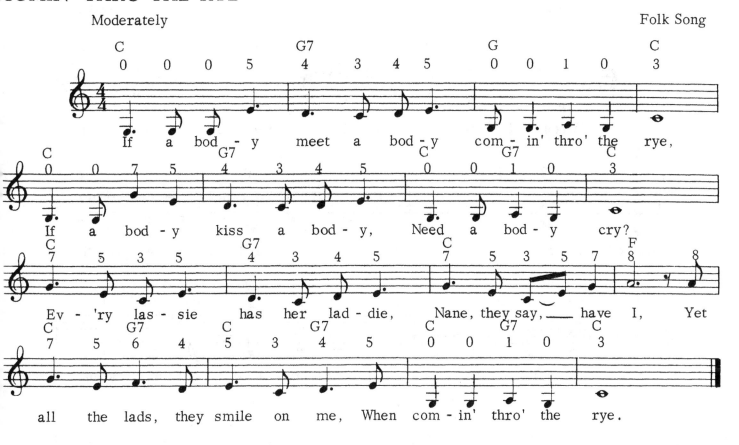

If a bod-y meet a bod-y com-in' thro' the rye,

If a bod-y kiss a bod-y, Need a bod-y cry?

Ev-'ry las-sie has her lad-die, Nane, they say,___ have I, Yet

all the lads, they smile on me, When com-in' thro' the rye.

HAIL, HAIL, THE GANG'S ALL HERE

Lively

Traditional

Hail, hail,___ the gang's all here! What the heck do

we care, What the heck do we care, Hail, hail,___ the

gang's all here, What the heck do we care now?___

THE FOGGY FOGGY DEW

Moderately

Folk Song

When I was a bach - 'lor, I lived all a - lone, I

worked at the weav - er's trade,_____ And the on - ly on - ly

thing I did that was wrong Was to woo a fair young

maid._____ I wooed___ her in the win - ter - time,___ And

in ___ the sum - mer too, _____ And the

on - ly on - ly thing that I did that was wrong, Was to

keep her from the fog - gy fog - gy dew._____

CARRY ME BACK TO OLD VIRGINNY

Moderately

JAMES A. BLAND

Car - ry me back to ol' Vir - gin - ny,

That's where the cot - ton and the corn and 'ta - ters grow.

There's where the birds war - ble sweet in the Spring - time,

There's where this old dark - ey's heart am long to go.

There's where I la - bor'd so hard for old Mas - sa, Day af - ter

day in the field of yel - low corn. No place on earth do I

love more sin - cere - ly, Than ol' Vir - gin - ny, the State where I was born.

PAPER ROSES

Moderately

TORRE & SPIELMAN

Copyright MCMLX by Pambill Music Inc.
Copyright assigned MCMLXII to Lewis Music Publishing Co. Inc.

POLLY WOLLY DOODLE

THE SLOOP JOHN B

Moderate calypso

Traditional

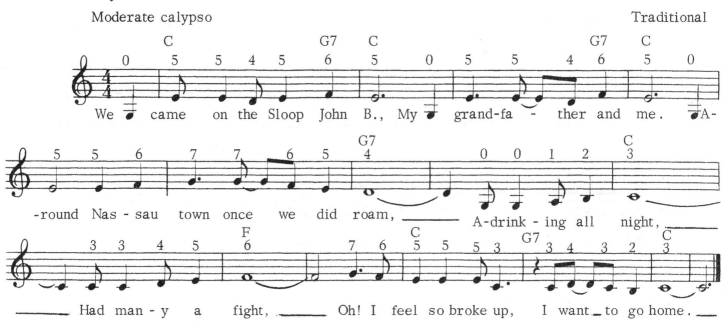

We came on the Sloop John B., My grand-fa - ther and me. A-round Nas - sau town once we did roam, _____ A-drink - ing all night, _____ Had man - y a fight, _____ Oh! I feel so broke up, I want _ to go home. _____

COCKLES AND MUSSELS

Moderate

Irish Folk Song

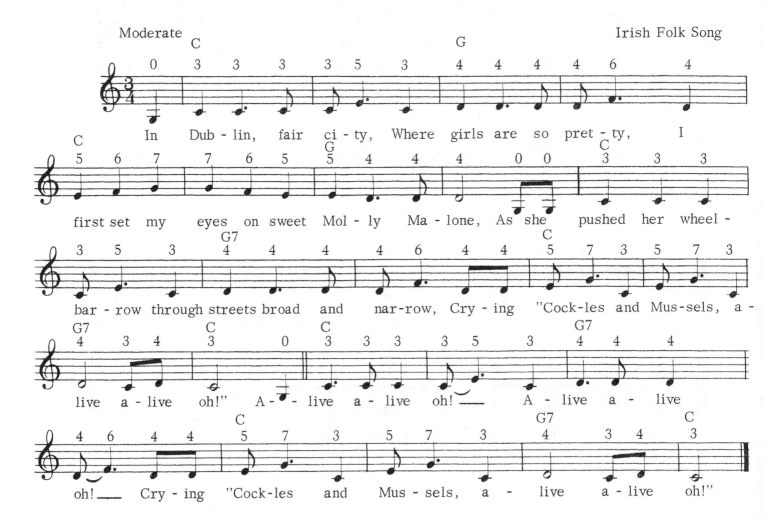

In Dub - lin, fair ci - ty, Where girls are so pret - ty, I first set my eyes on sweet Mol - ly Ma - lone, As she pushed her wheel - bar - row through streets broad and nar-row, Cry - ing "Cock-les and Mus-sels, a - live a - live oh!" A - live a - live oh! ____ A - live a - live oh! ___ Cry - ing "Cock-les and Mus - sels, a - live a - live oh!"

THE BLUE BELLS OF SCOTLAND

Scottish Folk Song

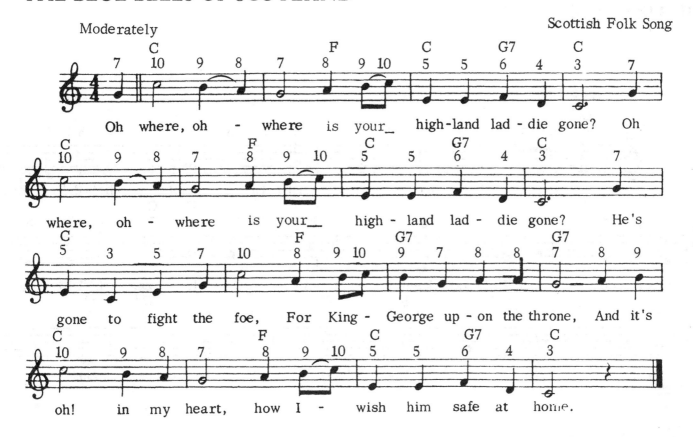

E WEARING OF THE GREEN

Irish Folk Song

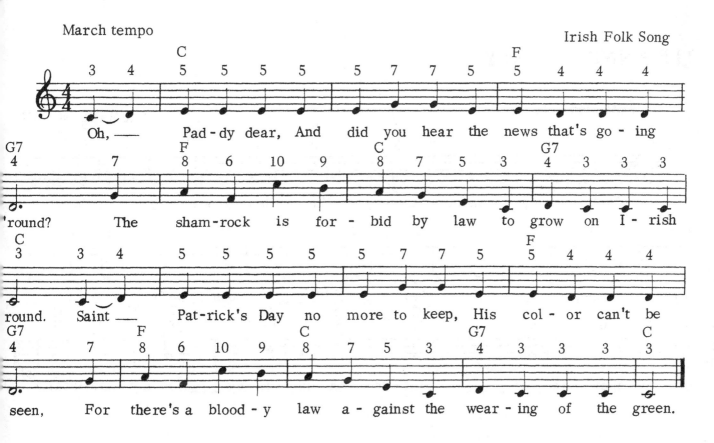

L'IL LIZA JANE

LITTLE ANNIE ROONEY

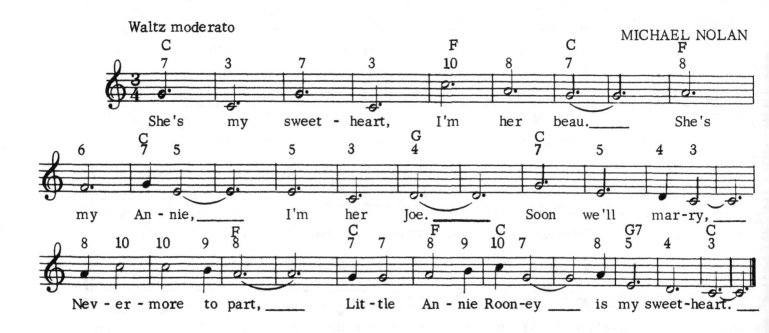

'ROUND HER NECK SHE WEARS A YELLOW RIBBON

Folk Song

IT'S HARD, AIN'T IT HARD?

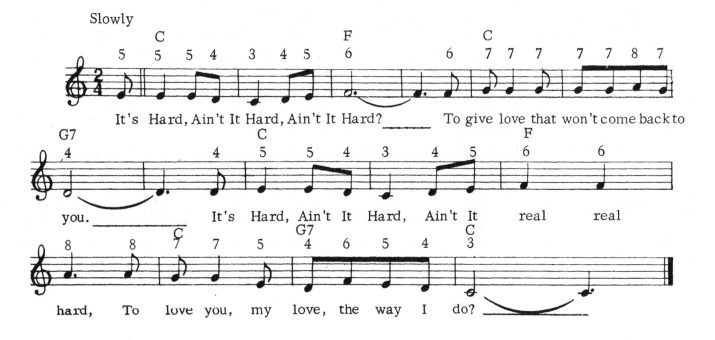

OLD FOLKS AT HOME

Moderately slow

STEPHEN FOSTER

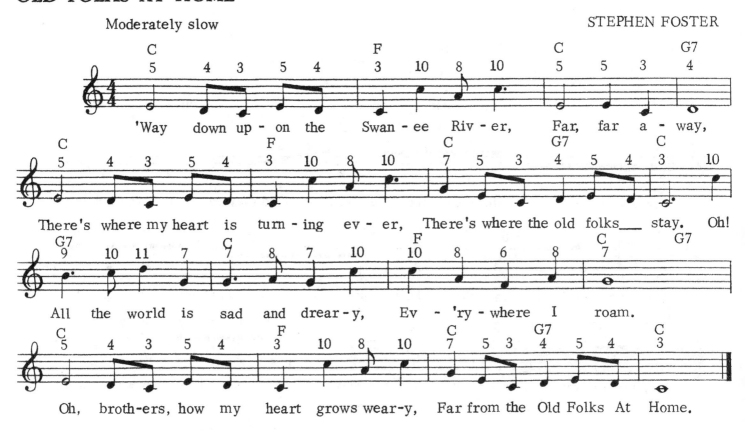

'Way down up - on the Swan - ee Riv - er, Far, far a - way,

There's where my heart is turn - ing ev - er, There's where the old folks___ stay. Oh!

All the world is sad and drear - y, Ev - 'ry - where I roam.

Oh, broth - ers, how my heart grows wear - y, Far from the Old Folks At Home.

OH! SUSANNA

STEPHEN FOSTER

Brightly

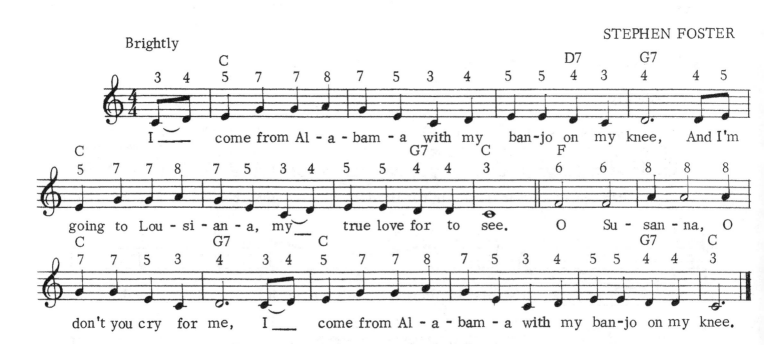

I___ come from Al - a - bam - a with my ban - jo on my knee, And I'm

going to Lou - si - an - a, my___ true love for to see. O Su - san - na, O

don't you cry for me, I___ come from Al - a - bam - a with my ban - jo on my knee.

SHORTNIN' BREAD

Brightly

Folk Song

Put on the skil-let, Put on the lead, Mam-my's gon-na make a lit-tle short-nin' bread.— That's not all— she's gon-na do,— She is gon-na make a lit-tle cof-fee, too.— CHORUS: Mam-my's lit-tle ba-by loves short-nin' short-nin' Mam-my's lit-tle ba-by loves short-nin' bread,— Mam-my's lit-tle ba-by loves short-nin' short-nin', Mam-my's lit-tle ba-by loves short-nin' bread.

REUBEN AND RACHEL

Moderately

Folk Song

1. (She) Reu-ben, Reu-ben, I've been think-ing, Life is some-times awf'-ly queer, No-one knows where we are go-ing, No-one knows why we are here.

2. (He) Rachel, Rachel, I've been thinking,
Those are true words that you've said.
Sleep all night when we are living,
Sleep all day when we are dead.

RHYTHM EFFECTS:

As a rule, you strum the strings with an inward sweep toward yourself. Each note is given one strum, covering all strings, pulling the pick inward.

As you advance in your technical ability, you may like to use extra strokes to produce a better rhythmic effect. These extra strokes must SUPPLEMENT but not INTERFERE with the basic rhythm of the selection.

Arrow points down ↓ : Stroke toward yourself. Arrow points up ↑ : Stroke away from yourself.

THE CAMPTOWN RACES

I GAVE MY LOVE A CHERRY
(The Riddle Song)

Folk Song

Moderately

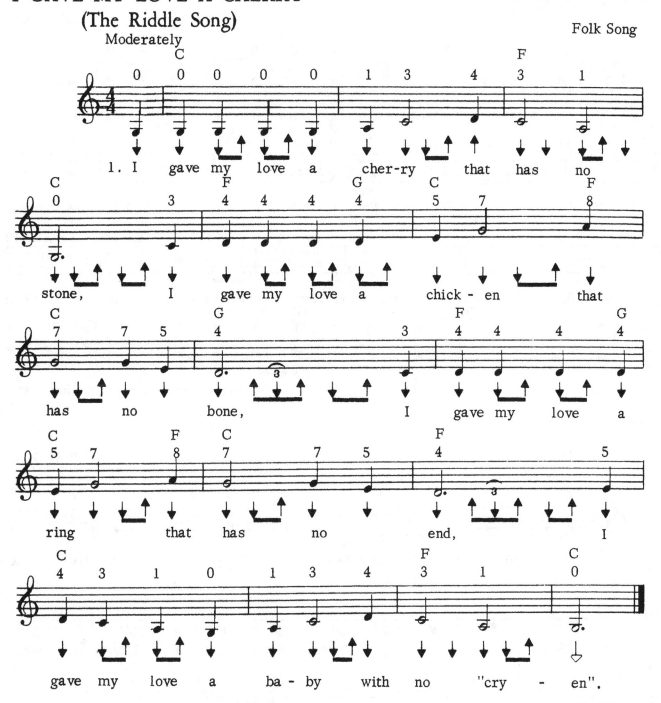

1. I gave my love a cher-ry that has no stone, I gave my love a chick - en that has no bone, I gave my love a ring that has no end, I gave my love a ba - by with no "cry - en".

2. How can there be a cherry that has no stone?
   How can there be a chicken that has no bone?
   How can there be a ring that has no end?
   How can there be a baby with no "cryen"?

3. A cherry when it's blooming, it has no stone,
   A chicken when it's pipping, it has no bone.
   A ring when it's rolling, it has no end,
   A baby, when it's sleeping, has no "cryen".

LITTLE BROWN JUG

Folk Song

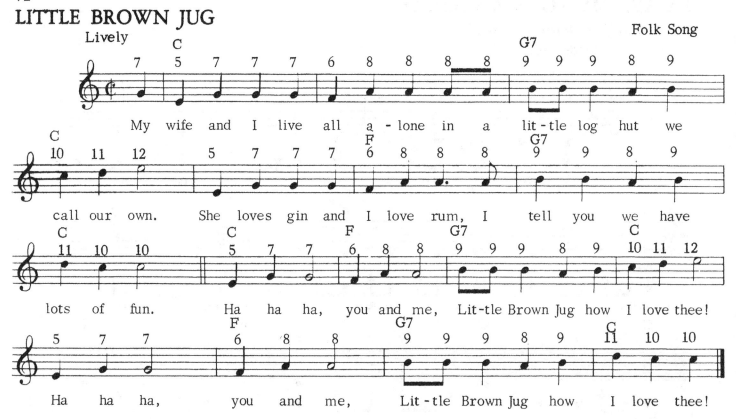

My wife and I live all a - lone in a lit - tle log hut we call our own. She loves gin and I love rum, I tell you we have lots of fun. Ha ha ha, you and me, Lit - tle Brown Jug how I love thee! Ha ha ha, you and me, Lit - tle Brown Jug how I love thee!

CINDY

Folk Song

1. I wish I was an ap - ple, A - hang - in' in a tree, And ev - 'ry time that Cin - dy passed, She'd take a bite of me.

Chorus:
Get a - long home, Cin - dy, Cin - dy, Get a - long home, Get a - long home, Cin - dy, Cin - dy, I'll mar - ry you some time.

2. I wish I had a quarter for ev'ry gal I know,
   But Cindy is the best of all, that's why I love her so. (Repeat Chorus)

3. I love her in the Springtime, I love her in the Fall,
   But all year 'round is just the time I love her most of all. (Repeat Chorus)

SOURWOOD MOUNTAIN

Moderately

Folk Song

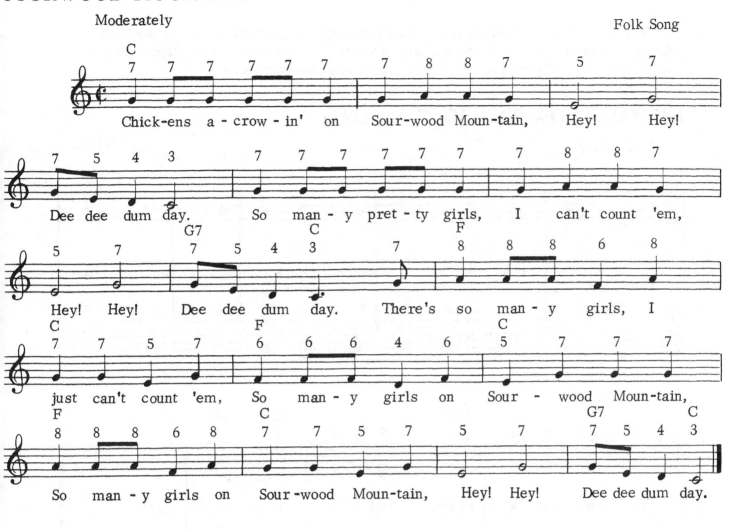

2. I call my darling a blue eyed daisy,
   Hey! Hey! Dee dee dum day.
   If she won't have me I'll sure go crazy,
   Hey! Hey! Dee dee dum day.
   I got to have my blue eyed daisy,
   If she refuses, I'll go crazy,
   I got to have my blue eyed daisy,
   Hey! Hey! Dee dee dum day.

3. Ducks go a-swimmin' across the river,
   Hey! Hey! Dee dee dum day,
   And in the winter we sure do shiver,
   Hey! Hey! Dee dee dum day.
   Ducks go a-swimmin' across the river,
   And in the winter we sure do shiver.
   I like the living on Sourwood Mountain,
   Hey! Hey! Dee dee dum day.

THE DESCANT

A DESCANT is a superimposed counter melody, sung or played above the main theme. This provides a harmonic part, so that the selection may be played solo, sung in duet form by two voices, or as a duet with two dulcimers.

MICHAEL, ROW THE BOAT ASHORE

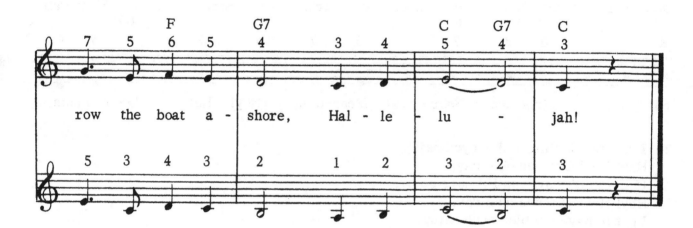

2. Sister, help to trim the sail, Hallelujah!
   Sister, help to trim the sail, Hallelujah!

3. Jordan River is chilly and cold, Hallelujah!
   Chills the body but not the soul, Hallelujah!

4. Jordan River is deep and wide, Hallelujah!
   Milk and honey on the other side, Hallelujah!

5. (Repeat)
   Michael, row the boat ashore, Hallelujah!
   Michael, row the boat ashore, Hallelujah!

KUM-BA-YA

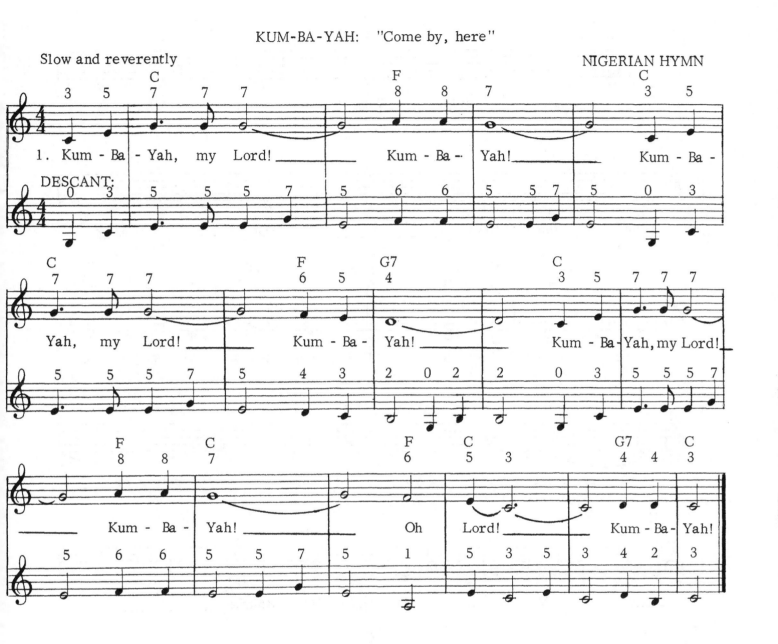

KUM-BA-YAH: "Come by, here"

Slow and reverently

NIGERIAN HYMN

2. Hear me crying, Lord, Kum-Ba-Yah! (Sing 3 times) ..... Oh Lord! Kum-Ba-Yah!

3. Hear me praying, Lord, Kum-Ba-Yah! (Sing 3 times) ..... Oh Lord! Kum-Ba-Yah!

4. Oh I need you, Lord, Kum-Ba-Yah! (Sing 3 times) .... Oh Lord! Kum-Ba-Yah!

THE SIDEWALKS OF NEW YORK

Moderate waltz

LAWLOR & BLAKE

AULD LANG SYNE

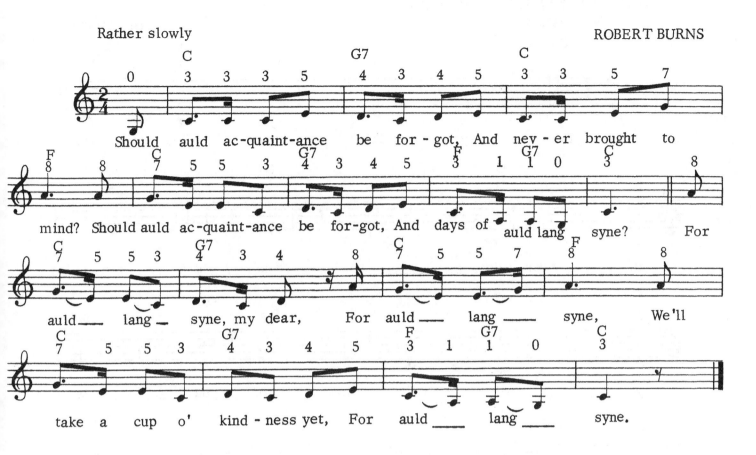

I LOVE YOU TRULY

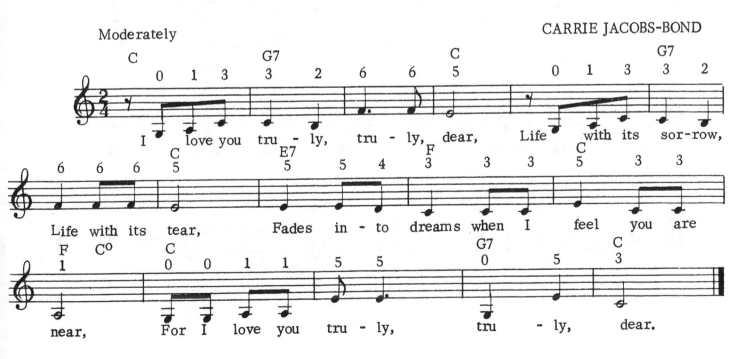

A BICYCLE BUILT FOR TWO

Moderate waltz

HARRY DACRE

UNDER THE BAMBOO TREE

IN THE GOOD OLD SUMMERTIME

COME ALL YE FAIR AND TENDER MAIDENS

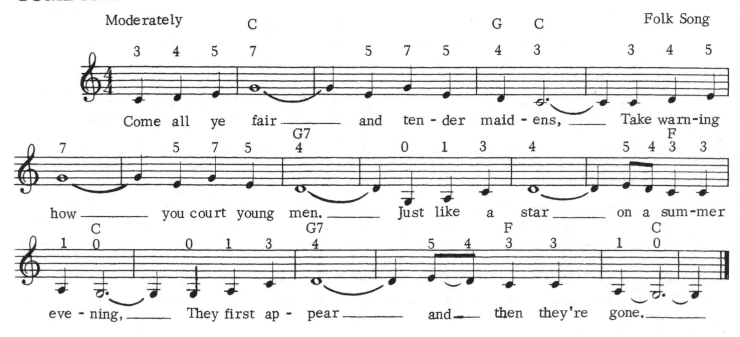

Come all ye fair ___ and ten-der maid-ens, ___ Take warn-ing how ___ you court young men. ___ Just like a star ___ on a sum-mer eve-ning, ___ They first ap-pear ___ and ___ then they're gone. ___

LOVE'S OLD SWEET SONG

BINGHAM and MOLLOY

Just a song at twi-light, When the lights are low, And the flick-'ring shad-ows soft-ly come and go, Tho' the heart be wea-ry, Sad the day and long, Still to us at twi-light, Comes love's old song, Comes love's ___ old sweet ___ song.

GIT ALONG, LITTLE DOGIES

Moderately

Cowboy Song

As I was a-walk-ing one morn-ing for plea-sure, I spied a cow punch-er a-rid-ing a-lone. His hat was thrown back and his spurs were a-jing-ling, And as he ap-proached, he was sing-ing this song: Whoop-ee ti, yi yo! Git a-long lit-tle do-gies, It's your mis-for-tune and none of my own. Whoop-ee ti, yi yo! Git a-long lit-tle do-gies, You know that Wy-om-ing will be your new home.

THE MINSTREL BOY

Moderately

Irish Song

1. The min-strel boy___ to the war has gone, In the ranks of death___ you'll___ find him. His fa-ther's sword___ he has gird-ed on, And his wild harp slung___ be-hind him. "Oh Land of Song" said the war-rior hard, "Tho' all the world be-trays___ thee, One sword, at least,___ thy___ rights will guard, One___ faith-ful harp___ will___ praise thee.

2. The minstrel fell,
But the foe's cruel chain
Could not bring that proud
   soul under,
The harp he loved
Never spoke again,
For he tore its chords
   asunder.
And said, "No chain shall
   sully thee,
Thou soul of love and bravery,
They songs were made for the
   pure and free,
They shall never sound in
   slav'ry."

3. The minstrel boy will return,
   we pray,
When we hear the news, we all
   will cheer it,
The minstrel boy will return
   one day,
Torn perhaps in body, not in
   spirit.
Then may he play on his harp
   in peace,
In a world such as Heaven has
   intended,
For all the bitterness of man
   must cease,
And ev'ry battle must be ended.

BELIEVE ME IF ALL THOSE ENDEARING YOUNG CHARMS

THOMAS MOORE

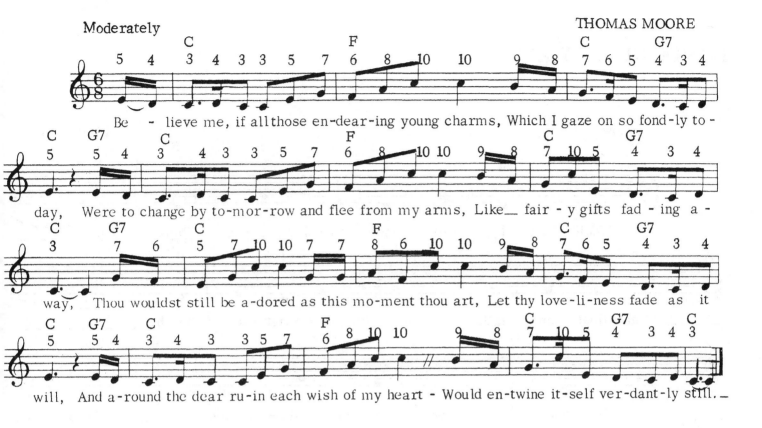

Be - lieve me, if all those en-dear-ing young charms, Which I gaze on so fond-ly to - day, Were to change by to-mor-row and flee from my arms, Like_ fair - y gifts fad-ing a - way, Thou wouldst still be a-dored as this mo-ment thou art, Let thy love-li-ness fade as it will, And a-round the dear ru-in each wish of my heart - Would en-twine it-self ver-dant-ly still. _

IN THE GLOAMING

ORED and HARRISON

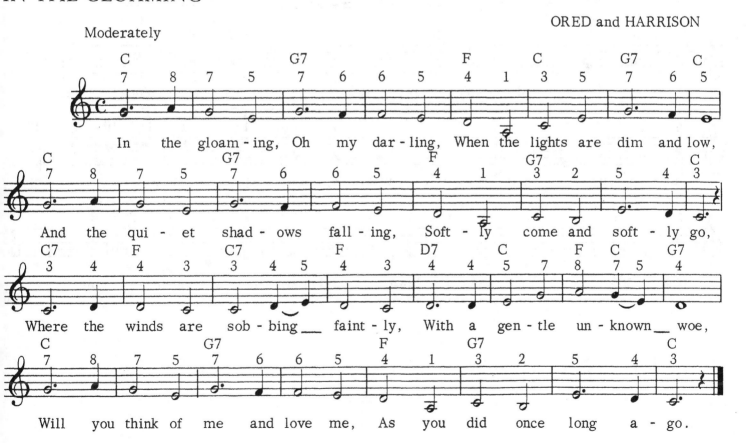

In the gloam-ing, Oh my dar-ling, When the lights are dim and low, And the qui-et shad-ows fall-ing, Soft-ly come and soft-ly go, Where the winds are sob-bing_ faint-ly, With a gen-tle un-known_ woe, Will you think of me and love me, As you did once long a - go.

LONDONDERRY AIR

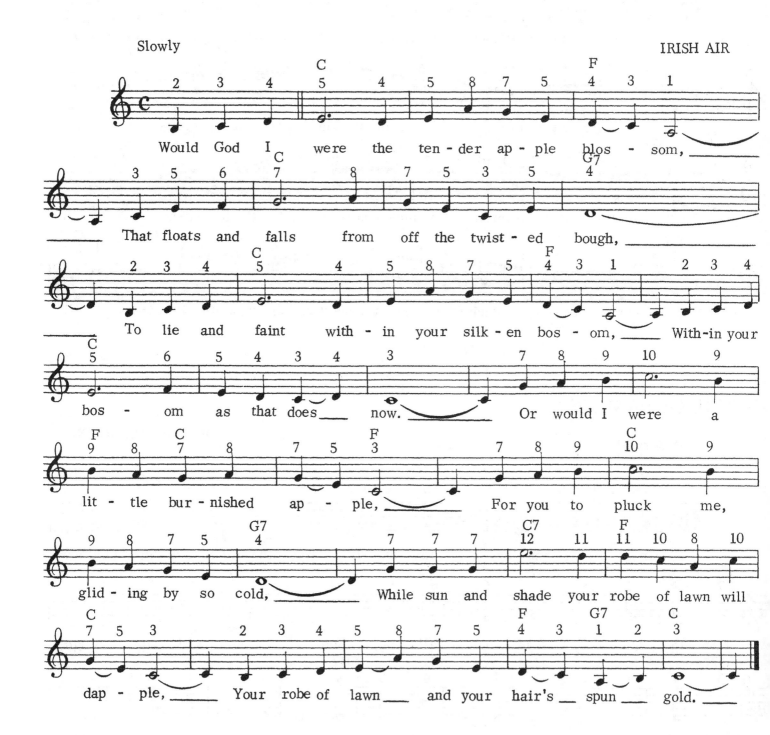

SWEET BETSY FROM PIKE

Moderate waltz

Folk Song

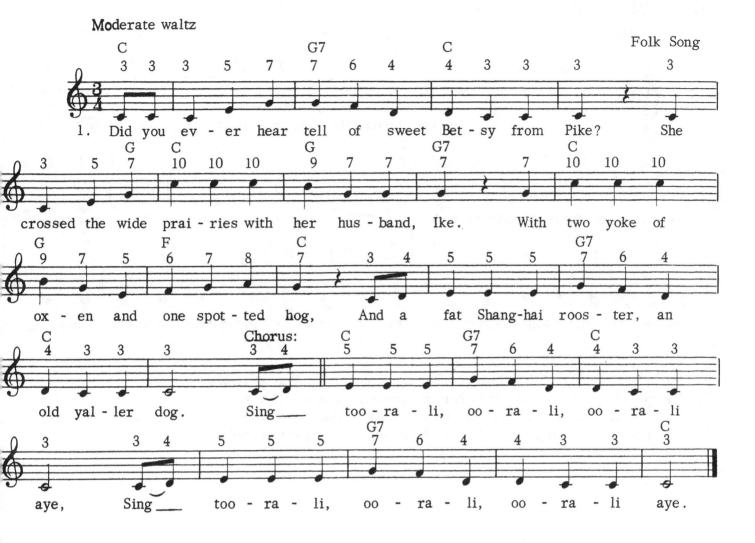

1. Did you ev-er hear tell of sweet Bet-sy from Pike? She crossed the wide prai-ries with her hus-band, Ike. With two yoke of ox-en and one spot-ted hog, And a fat Shang-hai roos-ter, an old yal-ler dog.

Chorus: Sing____ too-ra-li, oo-ra-li, oo-ra-li aye, Sing____ too-ra-li, oo-ra-li, oo-ra-li aye.

2. One evening quite early they camped by a stream.
To reach California, oh that was their dream.
The Shanghai was "et" but the cattle just died,
The last strip of bacon that morning was fried.   (Chorus)

3. Came the Injuns from nowhere, a wild yelling horde,
And Betsy was skeered as she prayed to the Lord.
Behind their big wagon the couple did crawl,
And they fought off the Injuns with musket and ball.   (Chorus)

4. Then they swam the wide rivers and crossed the tall peaks,
And lived on wild berries and water for weeks.
Starvation and hard work and sun-stroke as well,
But they reached California in spite of all hell.   (Chorus)

5. They were six months in Frisco, when Ike met a girl,
A sweet looking dancer who gave him a twirl.
He spoke of poor Betsy as "just an old horse",
What was Betsy to do? She gave Ike his divorce.   (Chorus)

6. She left Frisco and went back to Pike, so they say,
And Ike lost his dancer and soon passed away.
If this tale is touching, go cry if you like
Mighty fine kind of woman! Sweet Betsy from Pike.   (Chorus)

SHE'LL BE COMIN' 'ROUND THE MOUNTAIN

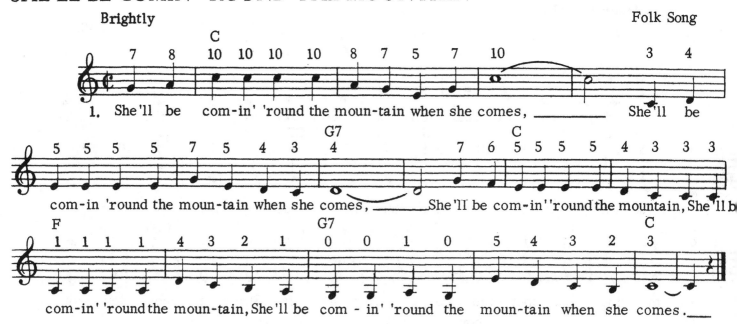

2. She'll be drivin' six white horses when she comes.   (Repeat to end)
3. We will all go out to meet her when she comes.   (Repeat to end)
4. We'll be singing "Hallelujah" when she comes.   (Repeat to end)
5. She'll be puffin' and a ·blowin' when she comes.   (Repeat to end)

OH! THEM GOLDEN SLIPPERS

FINGER PICKING

Illustrating "Finger Picking" discussed in introductory text. ③ This indicates fret pressed by left hand and melody string plucked by right hand. Diagonal line indicates a strum across strings 3-2-1. 3 lines below the staff represent the 3 strings of the dulcimer, picked in the strum hollow with right hand, in tempo and count indicated.

Place RH thumb against side of fingerboard near right hand end. Play with a slight lift in plucking motion. Index finger of RH plucks melody string and 2nd string. 3rd string - middle finger.

FINGER PICKING THE MAJOR SCALE:

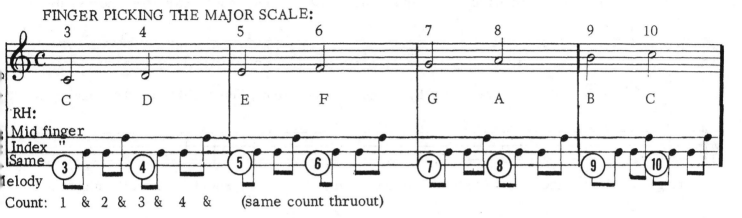

GOOD-NIGHT, LADIES

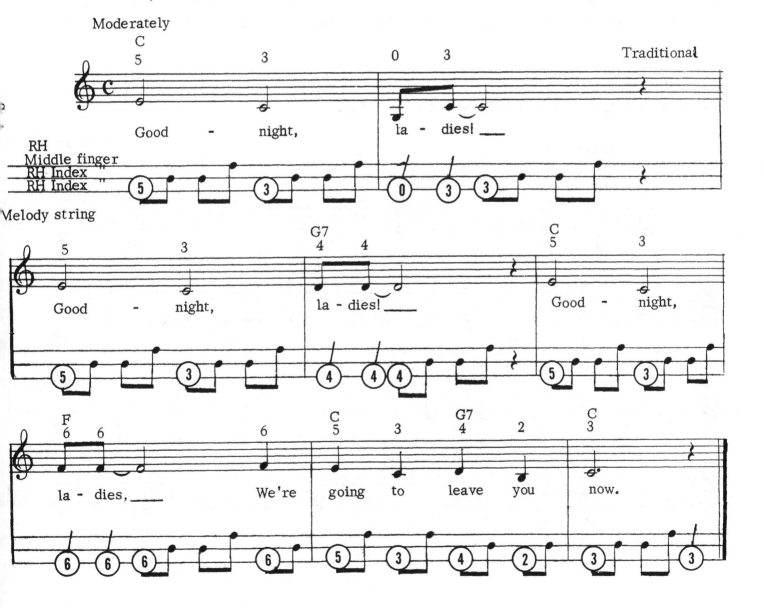

IN THE EVENING BY THE MOONLIGHT

JAMES A. BLAND

In the eve - ning by the moon-light, You could hear the peo - ple
sing-ing, In the eve - ning by the moon-light, You could hear the ban - jos
ring-ing, How the old folks would en - joy it, They would sit all night and
lis - ten, As we sang in the eve - ning by the moon - light.

THE MAN ON THE FLYING TRAPEZE

Traditional

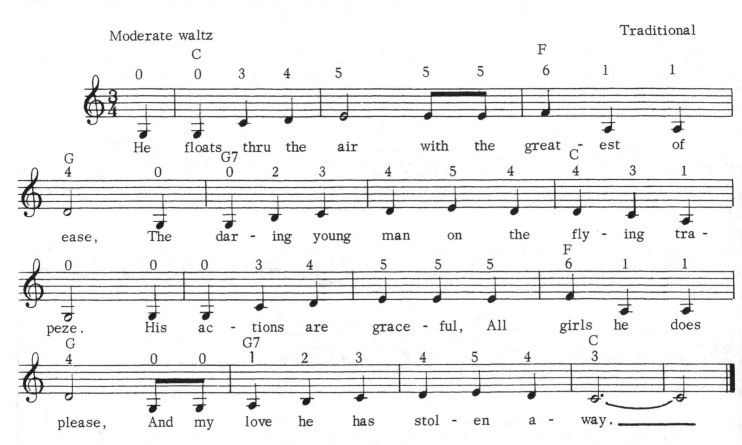

He floats thru the air with the great - est of
ease, The dar - ing young man on the fly - ing tra -
peze. His ac - tions are grace - ful, All girls he does
please, And my love he has stol - en a - way._____

MY WILD IRISH ROSE

Moderate waltz

CHAUNCEY OLCOTT

ANNIE LAURIE

Moderately

Scottish Song

WHEN YOU WERE SWEET SIXTEEN

JAMES THORNTON

THE CRAWDAD SONG

Folk Song

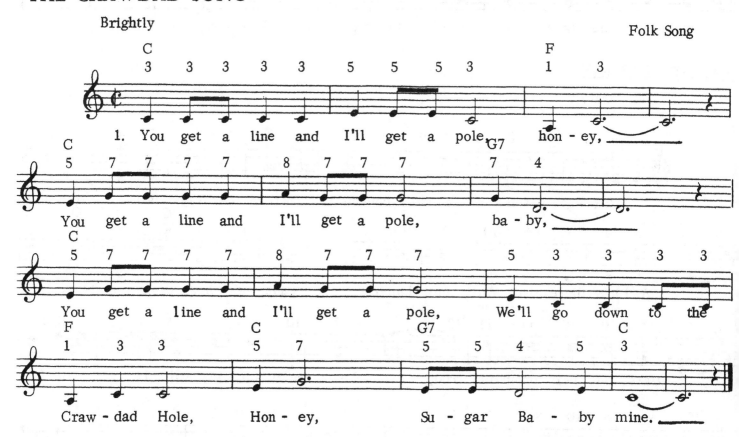

2. What'll you do if the creek goes dry, Honey?
What'll you do if the creek goes dry, Baby?
What'll you do if the creek goes dry?
Just sit down on the bank and cry,
Honey, Sugar Baby mine.

3. What'll you do when I'm old and gray, Honey?
What'll you do when I'm old and gray, Baby?
What'll you do when I'm old and gray?
Say, "Old man, please stay away,"
Honey, Sugar Baby mine.

SONGS IN MINOR MODE

Reminder: To go from the major to the minor mode, press down on the 3rd string to the left of the 6th fret and sound the note. Tune the first string to this note, leaving the 2nd and 3rd strings as they were in the major tuning.

IMPORTANT! In the Minor Tuning, the scale will start at the FIRST, not the third fret with which you started a scale in major tuning. Therefore, the numbers above the notes will be different for minor tuning. See chart on Page 12.

You will note that low C will be numbered 1 in Minor Tuning, numbered 3 in Major Tuning.

BARBARA ELLEN

MINOR TUNING

In Scar-let Town, Where I was__ born, There a fair young
All in the mer - ry month of __ May, When the green buds

maid was__ dwell - in', Man-y a fine young man sent his
they were__ swell - in', Young__ Wil-liam Green on his

heart on the way To the love of Bar - b'ra El - len.
death - bed __ lay For the love of Bar - b'ra El - len.

BLACK IS THE COLOR OF MY TRUE LOVE'S HAIR

MINOR TUNING

Rather slow

Folk Song

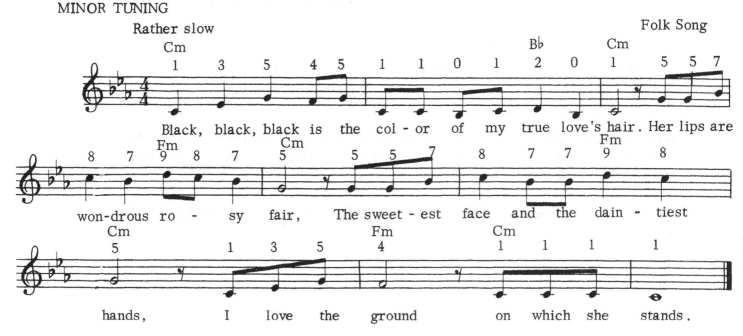

Black, black, black is the col - or of my true love's hair. Her lips are won-drous ro - sy fair, The sweet - est face and the dain - tiest hands, I love the ground on which she stands.

HATIKVOH

MINOR TUNING

Rather slowly

Hebrew Anthem

WHEN JOHNNY COMES MARCHING HOME

MINOR TUNING

Spirited march

Traditional

1. When John - ny comes march-ing home a - gain, Hur-rah!__ Hur-

rah! ___ We'll give him a heart - y wel - come then, Hur -

rah! Hur - rah! Oh the men will cheer and the

boys will shout, The la - dies, they__ will all turn out and we'll

all feel gay when John - ny comes march-ing home. ___

2. Oh Johnny, we say you've been away,
Too long, too long!
We welcome a hero home today,
With heart and song.
And ev'ryone in the town will cheer,
To show we're happy to have you here,
'Cause we'll feel that way,
When Johnny comes marching home.

3. Get ready to have a jubilee,
Hurrah! Hurrah!
Get ready with heart so light and free,
Hurrah! Hurrah!
A laurel wreath we have ready now,
To put in place on his loyal brow,
And we'll give three cheers,
When Johnny comes marching home.

4. When Johnny comes marching home again,
Hurrah! Hurrah!
A girlie will meet her man of men,
Hurrah! Hurrah!
That sweet young lady will head the crowd,
The first to kiss you and say she's proud
Of the man she loves,
When Johnny comes marching home.

I'M A POOR WAYFARIN' STRANGER

MINOR TUNING

Folk Song

2. I know dark clouds may gather 'round me,
   I know my way is dark and steep,
   But glorious fields lie just before me,
   Where God's redeemed, their vigil keep.
   I'm going there to see my Saviour,
   To sing His praises evermore,
   I'm just a-going over Jordan,
   I'm just a-going over home.

A SHIP WAS LOST AT SEA

MINOR TUNING

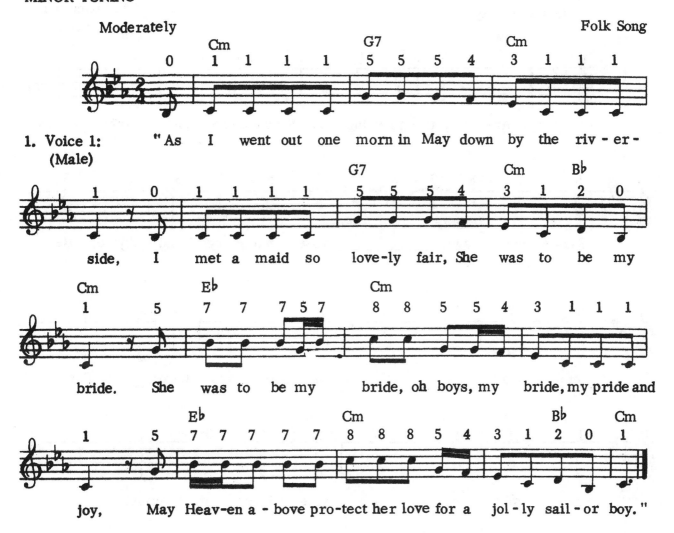

Moderately

Folk Song

1. Voice 1: (Male) "As I went out one morn in May down by the riv-er-side, I met a maid so love-ly fair, She was to be my bride. She was to be my bride, oh boys, my bride, my pride and joy, May Heav-en a-bove pro-tect her love for a jol-ly sail-or boy."

2. Voice 2: (Male or Female)

A father to his daughter said:
"What makes you so lament?
A sailor lad is coming here
To make your heart content."
"There is no lad a-coming here,
No sailor lad, said she,
The raging winds and stormy seas
Took my love away from me."

3. Voice 3: (Female)

"No handkerchief shall bind my head,
No comb go thru my hair,
No candle light near fireside
To view my beauty fair,
For the tempest on a stormy day
Took my love away from me.
I lost my jolly sailor boy,
When a ship was lost at sea."

SCARBOROUGH FAIR

MINOR TUNING

Rather slowly

Folk Song
Adaptation by:
A. G.

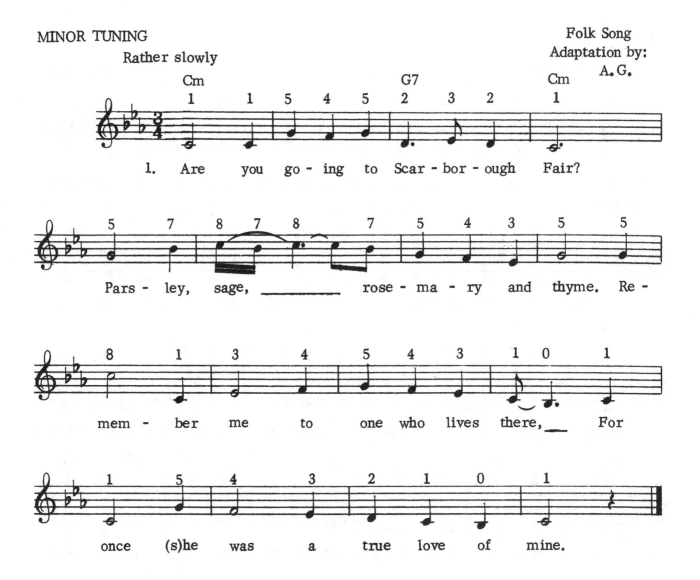

2. Have him make me a cambric shirt,
   Parsley, sage, rosemary and thyme,
   Without a seam or fine needlework,
   And then he'll be a true love of mine.

3. Have him wash it in yonder dry well,
   Parsley, sage, rosemary and thyme,
   Where ne'er a drop of water e'er fell,
   And then he'll be a true love of mine.

4. Have him find me an acre of land,
   Parsley, sage, rosemary and thyme,
   Between the sea and over the sand,
   And then he'll be a true love of mine.

5. Plow the land with the horn of a lamb,
   Parsley, sage, rosemary and thyme,
   Sow it with seeds from north of the dam,
   And then he'll be a true love of mine.

6. If he tells me he can't, I'll reply:
   Parsley, sage, rosemary and thyme,
   Let me know that at least he will try,
   And then he'll be a true love of mine.

7. Love imposes impossible tasks,
   Parsley, sage, rosemary and thyme,
   Though not more than any heart asks
   And I must know he's a true love of mine.